Terrier + Bulldog = PITBULL

Living with a
Jack Russell
Terrier

Edited by
Rani MorningStar

BARRON'S

Photo courtesy: Linda Miller.

First edition for the United States and Canada published
2000 by Barron's Educational Series, Inc.

All inquiries should be addressed to:

Barron's Educational Series, Inc.
250 Wireless Boulevard
Hauppauge, NY 11788
http://www.barronseduc.com

International Standard Book Number: 0-7641-5261-0

Library of Congress Catalog Card No: 00-101231

Printed in Singapore

9 8 7 6 5 4 3 2 1

CONTENTS

CHAPTER ONE

INTRODUCING THE JACK RUSSELL TERRIER

The Jack Russell Terrier needs little introduction. He is the lively little dog from Devon, England, who has become one of the most popular breeds in the Western world. Loving and loveable, he is utterly loyal to his owner and has the tough terrier temperament to boot.

RELIGIOUS ROOTS

The history of many breeds is shrouded in mystery and conjecture, but, being under 200 years of age, the Jack Russell's origins are fairly well documented. This is especially helped by the breed bearing the name of its creator: the Reverend John (Jack) Russell.

John Russell was born at Belmont House in Dartmouth, Devon, on December 21, 1795. After some years in Cornwall, the Russell family returned to Devon, and, after attending Plympton Grammar School, John Russell attended Blundell's school at Tiverton. It was here that he became friends with a pupil called

Robert Bovey, who shared Russell's love of hunting. Together, they worked a successful pack of Foxhounds, but their success was to be their downfall: Their reputation spread, eventually reaching their headmaster, who expelled Bovey, and gave Russell a thorough beating.

Russell's love of hunting continued nevertheless throughout his academic career. In 1814 he earned a scholarship to Exeter College, Oxford, but his studies did not prevent him from pursuing his love of wrestling, boxing, and hunting.

Trump the Terrier

In Russell's final year at Oxford University, there was a chance meeting that changed the course of canine history. Russell was walking in Marston, Oxford, looking for somewhere pleasant to sit and study the classic writer Horace.

Russell's biographer, fellow parson E.W.L. Davies, tells the story:

A milkman met him with a terrier—such an animal as Russell had yet only seen in his dreams; he halted, as Actaeon might have done when he caught sight of Diana disporting in her bath, but unlike that ill-fated hunter, he never budged from the spot till he had won the prize and secured it as his own. She was called Trump, and became the progenitress of that famous race of terriers that, from that day to the present, have been associated with Russell's name at home and abroad.

Russell considered Trump to be the ideal terrier, saying, "Her whole appearance gave indications of courage, endurance, and hardihood." His subsequent breeding programs all worked at maintaining this feisty working type.

A portrait of Trump that was painted in 1820, just a few months after Russell acquired her, shows a white dog with a dark tan patch over both eyes and ears, with a spot of color also at the base of the tail. She had a thick, wiry coat to protect her from the elements. Biographer

Davies describes the legs as being "straight as an arrow," and compares her size to that of a fox.

Trump was the founding bitch of Russell's breed of terrier, and, although there are no records of which dogs were mated to which bitches, it is known that Russell did not simply use dogs from his local area, but went in search of breeding stock from further away.

Work and Play

Russell's first position after being ordained was to become curate at George Nympton in Devon. He had a small pack of hounds with which he hunted otter in the summer, and fox in the winter, but, being a conscientious clergyman, he could not hunt as much as he wanted. It was not until he married Penelope Burn of Swimbridge, Devon, and moved to a less demanding position in Iddesleigh that he could spend more time hunting.

There was one occasion where Russell's love of hunting clashed with his pastoral duties. This occurred when the bishop heard reports that a child's funeral had been postponed, because it

Parson Russell's terriers were bred to be tough working dogs of great stamina and intelligence.

The terriers had to keep pace with hunters on horseback—today's dogs appear to have retained a special affinity with horses.

Photo courtesy: Rani MorningStar.

coincided with a hunt that Russell wanted to attend. The child's mother refused to make a complaint, however, and the matter was dropped.

John and Penelope Russell moved to Swimbridge in 1832, and Russell was to remain the parson there for 45 years. He was as devoted to his parishioners as they were to him.

Original Skills

During his time at Swimbridge, Russell's reputation for breeding terriers spread far and wide. His dogs had great stamina and intelligence, and were able to keep up with the hounds across the wild terrain of the moors, second-guessing where the quarry might bolt, and finding shortcuts to catch up with the hounds. It was said that Trump and her descendant, Tip, could run an exhausting 15 to 20 miles on a hunt.

The dogs were also bred to have good voices to signal the hounds should they find where the quarry had hidden. They were also bred to be tenacious and bold, to chase the quarry from any bolt holes so the chase could continue. It was never Russell's intention that the terriers should kill the fox.

Early Shows

By 1871, Russell—now in his mid-seventies—was finding it increasingly difficult to look after his terrier pack, so he passed it on to Henry Villebois, Master of the West Norfolk hunt. Having spent his entire life with his beloved terriers, Russell found a dogless existence quite unbearable, and it wasn't long before he had developed another small pack, more manageable in size.

Although he was not able to hunt as much as he used to, nor to keep as large a pack as he wanted, Russell's interest in dogs was still considerable, and, in 1873 he became one of the original founders of the British Kennel Club, judging terriers at the first sanctioned show in 1874.

Russell did not show his own dogs, believing there was too much difference between the show and working types. He described the difference between the types as being similar to that of a wildflower and a garden rose. Certainly, the Fox Terrier that Russell knew and loved underwent quite a transformation in the show ring. The breed's head became longer and narrower; a smooth coat was preferred in the ring; and a straight shoulder blade was developed, together with a wider chest. To many hunting enthusiasts, this new strain no longer had the physical ability to root out game, so they maintained their own type, which is still distinctly different from the Fox Terrier we have today.

Leaving Swimbridge

Penelope died in 1875, after 50 years of marriage, and soon after, Russell fell on hard times financially. Lord Poltimore, a hunting associate and an admirer of Russell's dedication to the church, came up with a solution to his problems by offering him a job at Black Torrington in Devon. Although the post involved a considerable increase in money, it meant Russell had to leave Exmoor—the area he knew and loved. It was a very difficult decision for Russell, but, in 1879 he made the move to his new parish.

More heartbreak was to follow when, shortly after moving, Russell's stables caught fire, killing his horses and kennelled dogs.

Russell died in 1883, and his remaining dogs were adopted by a variety of friends and hunting colleagues, though records detailing exactly what happened to his stock do not exist.

THE BREED'S PROGRESS

If John Russell is the father of the breed, then Arthur Heinemann can be considered the uncle, for he worked to keep the breed alive after the parson's death.

Heinemann was the secretary of the Parson Jack Russell Club, an organization set up in 1894 to safeguard the future of the working terrier at a time when the show Fox Terrier had changed so dramatically. The club was founded "to promote the breeding of the old-fashioned North Devon type of Fox Terrier, as bred and made famous by Rev. J. Russell."

Heinemann was also a judge, and he judged the working Fox Terrier at the Crufts dog show in 1909, a class encouraging the original breed nurtured by Russell.

After Russell's death, a group of enthusiasts worked to keep the breed alive.

Heinemann acquired as many direct descendants from Russell's stock as he could. He then bred to maintain the type, and wrote a Breed Standard for others to follow too. Unfortunately, Heinemann's passion for badger digging meant that not all his stock remained pure.

Not to be confused with badger baiting, badger digging involved a terrier finding a badger that had buried itself, so the handler could dig it out, put it in a bag, weigh it, and release it. The "sport" required a dog that was stronger and tougher, and Heinemann is believed to have introduced some Bull Terrier blood to his lines to achieve this. The wider head can still be seen in some strains today.

Rise and Fall

During World War II, the working-type Parson Jack Russell Terrier suffered quite a decline, as many breeds did, and the Parson Jack Russell Terrier Club eventually closed. However, the postwar years saw the emergence of the short-legged Jack Russell Terrier, which is still a very popular pet, though very distinct from the original Parson terrier. Many were crossed with such dogs as the Chihuahua, the Yorkie, and even the Corgi, as well as to other types of terriers, such as the Lakeland, the Fox Terrier, and the Staffordshire Bull Terrier, without official recognition from the American or British Kennel Clubs; there was no control over what breeds were introduced into the short-legged Jack Russell.

The emergence of the short-legged Jack Russell has led to much controversy within the breed.

The Parson Jack Russell Terrier, in the meantime, was still being bred mainly by enthusiasts in Devon, and the Parson Jack Russell Terrier Club eventually reemerged in 1983 after owners and breeders became concerned for their breed's future. The threat this time was not the show Fox Terrier, but the increasingly popular short-legged Jack Russell. The Parson Jack Russell was officially recognized by the British Kennel Club in 1990, but, because of continued confusion with the other types of Jack Russell, the "Jack" was dropped in 1999, and the breed became known as the Parson Russell Terrier. The Parson Jack Russell Terrier Breed Standard is based on the one for the original Fox Terrier, drafted by Heinemann.

As well as the pet Jack Russell, the other type that is often confused with the Parson, is the working-type Jack Russell Terrier. A sturdy, tough terrier, the working Jack Russell Terrier bears a very close resemblance to the Parson. The main difference is size—the ideal Parson is 14 inches (36 cm) to the shoulder, whereas the working Jack Russell can be between 10 and 15 inches (25–38 cm).

The Jack Russell name has caused similar confusion in many countries around the world. Australia, for example, has the Parson Jack Russell Terrier and the Australian Jack Russell. In America, a copyright on the name Parson Jack Russell Terrier means that although the dogs are very similar to the British Parsons, the breed has to be called the Jack Russell Terrier instead. Even Parson Jack Russell Terriers, who, before the British name change, were exported from Britain to America, could no longer be registered as Parsons, but rather as Jack Russell Terriers.

THE BREED TODAY

Whatever the name, all three types of Jack Russell have a similar personality. A tenacious little character, and a true survivor, it is not surprising that the breed is so popular today—in all its forms! Despite changes in hunting trends that led to other breeds being used in the field, the Jack Russell still found a place in people's homes. Of course, there are still working Jack Russells, but the majority are well-loved pets.

Today the Jack Russell is one of the most popular of pet dogs—his greatest joy is to join in with family activities.
Photo courtesy: Debbie Harrison.

The Jack Russell is now one of the most popular breeds in the United Kingdom and the United States, and it is easy to understand why. He is a big dog in a small body, and lives life to the fullest. A convenient size to house, feed, and transport, the Jack Russell is a go-getter, full of fun and mischief. Because of this, he needs an equally strong-willed owner to cope with his endless antics, and his larger-than-life personality.

TERRIER TELEPATHY

Many families with a Jack Russell report how the dog seems to have extrasensory perception. Certainly, like most dogs that develop close bonds with their owners, the Jack Russell has a remarkable talent for tuning into his owner's moods—of acting the clown when the owner needs cheering up, or becoming quiet and affectionate when a cuddle is really needed. However, the Jack Russell's talent does not always stop there, as these owners report.

Pain Relief

"When I got Milo, I was very impressed with the bond that formed between us so early. Milo followed me everywhere and was therefore in tune with my every move and emotion. I started noticing small instances of me thinking something and Milo reacting to that thought. For instance, I would think: 'I need to give him a bath,' would turn around and not be able to find him—he would be hiding under the couch. I can run myself a bath and he comes to lie on my clothes, but he knows when the bath is for him, even before I do anything different.

"The most recent event, that I will never forget, happened this year. Milo is not very demonstrative of his affections. He greets me very happily when I get home, but then gets on my lap and lays facing away from me. That is his way of being close.

"This year, I had back surgery and wasn't doing too well. I went to a pain management center for injections and was feeling even worse and in more pain. I was lying on the bed crying—and felt something moving on the bed. I looked down and Milo was slowly crawling toward me. He gently crawled up on my chest, tucked his front legs underneath him and laid his head gently on my face and would lick a tear and then lie across my face. He was pushing his head against my face as if to give me a hug. I just started to laugh, even through the pain. He had never done that before and it touched me to

The breed's special sensitivity has led to many owners feeling that their dogs have special extrasensory powers.

know that he knew I was hurting and was so incredibly gentle."
Teresa York, Texas

Diabetes Alert

"My husband had diabetes, and our dog, Tess, could foretell when he was having an insulin reaction. Sometimes she would come up to him while he was sitting watching TV and would bark at him or poke him with her nose. She would try to get him into the kitchen—she knew that he needed to eat.

"One time, she went to the door and sat and whined as if somebody was approaching the house. My husband soon walked in the door, even though he wasn't expected. He also wasn't driving one of our cars—a friend from his work had brought him home due to a reaction."
Laurel Pierson, Oregon

Quake Predictions

"There were several times that our dog, Hanna, acted really edgy and nervous for a couple of days, and then would settle back into her relatively laid-back disposition. It finally occurred to us what was happening, and when we looked at the calendar, it was confirmed. All of those 'nervous' incidents preceded an earthquake by one to two days."
Paul Gerris, California

Phone Home

"Our dog, Scat, was really attached to my husband and could foresee when he was going to telephone. When my husband occasionally had to make trips out of town, it was not unusual for Scat to run from the room she was in, jump on the table that the phone was on, and just wait for it to ring. Sure enough, it would ring and it would be my husband."
Janet Copeland, California

Sixth Sense

"I remember when Jackie didn't recognize my father the three days before he passed away. This little dog would normally lick my father for hours at a time. Jackie had a closeness to people who needed that extra attention. She had an intuition that was unbelievable to most humans.

"Well, just before Dad passed away (he hadn't eaten in several days), I had him to our house, hoping that he would eat dinner. I tried to talk to him, but Jackie wouldn't let us talk—she growled and paced back and forth wanting the 'stranger' to leave. We think that she knew that Dad had already begun to leave.

"It was so sad when he died; I was with him and when I came home that night, it was really interesting how Jackie wouldn't leave my side, and, when I cried, she cried too."
Dianna Eaton, Washington.

CHAPTER TWO

PUPPY POWER

ll puppies are cute, but Jack Russell puppies are utterly irresistible. They are mischievous and playful, and, being the fun-loving dogs they are, you are likely to spend much of their puppyhood laughing at their antics. There will be times, however, when you will feel like tearing your hair out. Our puppy survival guide will help you through the good times and the bad.

FINDING THE RIGHT PUPPY

Buying a dog should be a well-thought-out process. You should ask yourself the following questions:

- Can I afford a dog, and his veterinary care?
- Do I have a lifestyle suited to dog ownership?
- Do my work commitments allow me to have a dog?
- Do I have the time to exercise and groom him regularly?

- Am I prepared to dedicate time to training him?
- Can I cope with dog hairs and muddy paws in the house and in the car?
- Am I prepared to look after a dog for the next 14 years or so?
- Do I have a suitable home and garden?

Once you are sure you can be a responsible dog owner, you have to decide what type of dog you want. If you want a quiet, sedentary lapdog, the Jack Russell Terrier is not the breed for you. He is active and energetic, and needs an owner who will offer discipline and leadership, and who can meet his exercise requirements (at least two half-hour periods every day).

Buyer Beware

If you are certain you can give a Jack Russell a happy home and the right lifestyle, you will have to find a responsible breeder. The Jack Russell is a popular breed, and this is often exploited by puppy farms ("mills") that churn

out dogs for profit, with little care for the consequences. Dogs from puppy farms are usually poor quality and often have inferior temperaments too. Little if no thought goes into their breeding, and many hereditary conditions are rife in puppy-farmed dogs.

To avoid expensive veterinary or training bills, and possible heartbreak later on, you should "grill" the breeder. A responsible breeder will not mind being questioned—and will probably interrogate you, too! A good breeder will offer after-sales advice for the whole of the dog's life, and most will offer to take him back if any unforeseen problems occur.

"A dominant dog will run rings around a novice owner."

The litter should be raised in the home, as the puppies will then grow up well socialized to ordinary household noises (such as the washing machine or vacuum cleaner) and will be used to interacting with people. You should be given the opportunity to see the mother of the puppies, and she should be healthy and have an amiable temperament. You should also ask about the dam's and the sire's history to ensure there are no hereditary problems which may surface later in the pups. (See Chapter Nine, Health Care.)

Picking a Puppy

Once you are satisfied with the breeder, you can turn your attention to the puppies. It is a mistake even to look at the litter before this, as you may end up making a decision with your heart rather than with your head.

If you want only a single animal, it makes little difference if you have a male or female dog. Both make affectionate, loyal pets. The only difference is physical—females are slightly smaller and, if you do not neuter, will have seasons (see page 55). However, the sex of the animal will be an important factor should you come to choose a second dog (see page 59). You may also have a preference as to whether you want a smooth-coated dog that requires minimal grooming care, or a rough or broken-coated dog that will need regular stripping (see page 65).

The final decision will be choosing the individual puppy. As well as looking for a clean, healthy pup, with bright eyes and a good coat, you should also pick a puppy with a personality to match your requirements and your experience with the breed.

A Jack Russell with a dominant personality will run rings around a novice pet owner who does not understand how to handle the breed. Spoiling your dog, and not being consistent in training and discipline will lead to problems. Dominant puppies are best left to those with experience with the breed, who have plenty of time for training. Such puppies benefit from a mentally stimulating environment, often excelling in Competitive Obedience, where they work closely with, and develop a healthy respect for, their owner. Someone with little experience with the breed needs a puppy with a more submissive attitude that will not try to challenge the established hierarchy.

THE PUPPY APTITUDE TEST

merican psychologist Wendy Volhard has devised a temperament test that is useful in ascertaining a puppy's character.

The tests are used for all breeds of dogs aged about eight weeks, but are particularly invaluable when dealing with a breed as dominant as the Jack Russell.

As American breeder Mary Strom says: "Jack Russells are real opportunists. They need structure in their lives, and if the owner does not show them they are the least important member in the family—the bottom of the pack—they will be running the household in no time."

SOCIAL ATTRACTION

Place puppy in test area. From a few feet away the tester coaxes the puppy to him/her by clapping hands gently and kneeling down. Tester must coax the puppy in a direction away from the point where it entered the testing area.

PURPOSE
Degree of social attraction, confidence or dependence.

SCORE
Came readily, tail up, jumped, bit at hands	1
Came readily, tail up, pawed, licked at hand	2
Came readily, tail up	3
Came readily, tail down	4
Came hesitantly, tail down	5
Didn't come at all	6

FOLLOWING

Stand up and walk away from the puppy in a normal manner.
Make sure the puppy sees you walk away.

PURPOSE
Degree of following attraction. Not following indicates independence.

SCORE
Followed readily, tail up, got underfoot, bit at feet	1
Followed readily, tail up, got underfoot	2
Followed readily, tail up	3
Followed readily, tail down	4
Followed hesitantly, tail down	5
Didn't follow, or went away	6

RESTRAINT
Crouch down and gently roll the puppy on his back and hold him with one hand for a full 30 seconds.

PURPOSE
Degree of dominant or submissive tendency.
How the puppy accepts stress when socially/physically dominated.

SCORE
Struggled fiercely, flailed, bit	1
Struggled fiercely, flailed	2
Settled, struggled, settled with eye contact	3
Struggled then settled	4
No struggle	5
No struggle, straining to avoid eye contact	6

SOCIAL DOMINANCE
Let the puppy stand up and gently stroke him from the head to the back, while you crouch beside him. Continue stroking until a recognizable behavior is established.

PURPOSE
Degree of acceptance of social dominance. Puppy may try to dominate by jumping and nipping, or is independent and walks away.

SCORE
Jumped, pawed, bit, growled	1
Jumped, pawed	2
Cuddled up to tester and tried to lick face	3
Squirmed, licked at hands	4
Rolled over, licked at hands	5
Went away and stayed	6

ELEVATION DOMINANCE
Bend over, cradle the puppy under his belly, fingers interlaced, palms up, and elevate him just off the ground. Hold him there for 30 seconds.

PURPOSE
Degree of acceptance dominance while in position of no control.

SCORE
Struggled fiercely, bit, growled	1
Struggled fiercely	2
No struggle, relaxed	3
Struggled, settled, licked	4
No struggle, licked at hands	5
No struggle, froze	6

At eight weeks, puppies already have their own distinct personalities, and it is important to try and select the pup that will suit your lifestyle.

INTERPRETING THE SCORES

Mostly 1s

A puppy consistently scoring a 1 in the temperament section of the test is an extremely dominant, aggressive puppy that can easily be provoked to bite. His dominant nature will attempt to resist human leadership, thus requiring only the most experienced of handlers. This puppy is a poor choice for most individuals and will do best in a working situation.

Mostly 2s

This puppy is dominant and self-assured. He can be provoked to bite; however, he readily accepts human leadership that is firm, consistent, and knowledgeable. This is not a dog for a tentative, indecisive individual. In the right hands, he has the potential to become a fine working or show dog, and could fit into an adult household, provided the owners know what they are doing.

Mostly 3s

The puppy is outgoing and friendly, and will adjust well in situations in which he receives regular training and exercise. He has a flexible temperament that adapts well to different types of environments, provided he is handled correctly. May be too much for a family with small children or for an elderly couple who is sedentary.

Mostly 4s

A puppy that scores a majority of 4s is an easily controlled, adaptable puppy whose submissive nature will make him continually look to his master for leadership. This puppy is easy to train, reliable with kids, and, though he lacks self-confidence, makes a high-quality family pet. He is usually less outgoing than a puppy scoring in the 3s, but his demeanor is gentle and affectionate.

Mostly 5s

This is a puppy that is extremely submissive and lacking in self-confidence. He bonds very closely with his owner and requires regular companionship and encouragement to bring him out of his shell. If handled incorrectly, this puppy will grow very shy and fearful. For this reason, he will do best in a predictable, structured lifestyle with owners who are patient and not overly demanding, such as an elderly couple.

Mostly 6s

A puppy that scores 6 consistently is independent and uninterested in people. He will mature into a dog that is not demonstrably affectionate and that has a low need for human companionship. In general, it is rare to see properly socialized puppies test this way; however, there are several breeds that have been bred for specific tasks (such as Basenjis, hounds, and some northern breeds) that can exhibit this level of independence. To perform as intended, these dogs require a singularity of purpose that is not compromised by strong attachments to their owner.

For most owners, a good companion dog will score in the 3 to 4 range in this test. Puppies scoring a combination of 1s and 2s require experienced handlers who will be able to draw the best aspects of their potential from them.

HOMEWARD BOUND

After picking the right Jack Russell pup for you, and having waited until the breeder is willing to let the puppies leave, you will be eager to get your new addition home. Make sure you are fully prepared for the trip and make it as comfortable as possible for the puppy. Jack

Russells are known to have very long memories, and have even been called "little elephants" because of this! If his first impression of his new life is a miserable one, it will take some time to rebuild his trust in you.

The best idea is to take a dog-loving friend along with you when you collect the pup. Ideally, ask your friend to drive and this will leave you free to give your full attention to your new Jack Russell. Take a towel to put on your lap and to mop up any accidents that may happen. Do not be too concerned if the puppy is sick; it is perfectly natural until he gets used to car travel (see page 37). However, it is preferable if the puppy is not sick, as he could go on to develop a phobia of car travel because of his unpleasant experience. To minimize the risk of carsickness, the breeder will probably

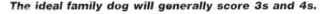

The ideal family dog will generally score 3s and 4s.

The waiting is over—the time has come to bring your puppy home.   **Photo courtesy: Rani MorningStar.**

make sure the puppy has an empty tummy before leaving. It is also advisable to make sure the puppy cannot see out of the window, as this can sometimes induce vomiting.

If it is a long trip, make sure the car interior does not get too hot, and make sure the puppy has water.

Settling In

When you get your Jack Russell puppy home, it will be difficult to restrain yourself from constantly cuddling him, but try not to wear him out. Puppies need lots of sleep, and, after being removed from his dam and littermates, and having endured the car journey, your Jack Russell may not be in an outgoing, playful frame of mind.

Once all the introductions to the family have been made, and the puppy has gotten over his

initial excitement of being somewhere new, take him outside to the yard to see if he will relieve himself. Feed him if he is due for a meal.

Turn a dog crate (see page 37) into a comfortable little den somewhere quiet (the kitchen is often a good choice), and settle him in it with a blanket and some chew toys. To ease the transition from breeder to owner, it is worth taking a blanket to the breeder's home a week or two before he is due to leave. The puppy will get used to the blanket, and, when you take him home, he will have a familiar item and scent around him to make him feel more confident.

The First Night

The first night can be difficult—so be prepared for very little sleep. Your Jack Russell puppy will be away from his littermates for the first time, and he will miss the comforting warmth of their bodies.

Take the puppy outside to relieve himself, and then settle him in the crate (so he can't endanger himself in the night by chewing through wires, etc.). It is a good idea to leave a radio on quietly in the room; some breeders recommend leaving a ticking clock nearby, which is said to be reassuring to pups, since it reminds them of their mother's heartbeat.

The puppy will probably start to cry as soon as he is left alone. Opinion is divided as to how you should respond to this. Some advise ignoring the cries, believing that if you always go to a puppy when he cries, it will encourage

Give the puppy a chance to explore the house— and the garden.

Photo courtesy: Rani MorningStar.

Your puppy is likely to feel bewildered to begin with.

The first night, separated from his littermates, may require some patience.

him to continue. Others believe that leaving the puppy in distress is cruel, and that comforting him back to sleep is a good way of establishing a trusting relationship.

However you respond, be cautious about taking the puppy to bed with you. It is a tempting solution when you are desperate for some sleep, but, once done, it is difficult to discourage the dog, especially one with as good a memory as the Jack Russell. You should also be aware that letting a dominant dog on the bed can send the wrong signals to the opportunist Jack Russell. Sharing the pack leader's bed may give the pup a false sense of

importance, resulting in complex problems further down the line.

The puppy may cry out in the early morning because he may need to go outside. In this case, it is only right to take him outside immediately. All puppies hate to soil near their sleeping quarters, and a prompt reaction will help house-training (see House-training, page 35.)

Feeding

When you purchase your Jack Russell puppy, the breeder will give you a diet sheet, and probably some food. It is very important to follow the diet sheet. If you wish to change the puppy's diet, it must be done very gradually. Puppies are prone to digestive upsets if their food is changed, so it is best to continue feeding what he is used to, making sure to stick to the measured amounts suggested by the breeder.

If the food does not agree with him, add a small amount of another brand to his food, gradually increasing the amount over a number of days, until an entire change has been made.

Puppies need to be fed at regular intervals throughout the day—usually four meals each day. Remember that a puppy has a lot of growing to do, and his body will need more energy than an adult dog. Over a period of time, the number of meals will need to be reduced. Gradually

It is advisable to stick to the food your puppy is familiar with while he is settling in.

increase the amounts (follow manufacturer's guidelines, or your breeder's diet sheet), and reduce the number of meals. As a general rule, the number of meals can be cut to three a day when the puppy is about four months old, and then to two a day at about six months of age.

If you are feeding a complete food (many special puppy varieties are available), you can soften the food with warm water or puppy milk, but make sure you allow it to cool before giving it to the puppy.

Soft stools can be a sign of overfeeding, so adjust the amount given accordingly. Of course, if the puppy has diarrhea, vomits, or loses interest in his food, you must seek veterinary advice at once.

CHAPTER THREE

EARLY LEARNING

O nce your Jack Russell has gotten over the trauma of changing homes, you need to start on his education—and the sooner you start, the better. The first step is to make sure that all relationships within the family get off on the right foot.

GETTING ALONG WITH CHILDREN

Terriers generally do not have the best reputation for being good with children, but, in the Jack Russell's case, this is not entirely deserved. Russells are not always the most patient dogs, and, being a dominant breed, they are sometimes unwilling to put up with being treated inconsiderately by children. Dogs from some lines can also be quick to snap. However, if you purchased your puppy from a reputable breeder, that has been bred as much for temperament as for conformation, the likelihood of problems arising is drastically reduced.

Good breeding lays solid foundations, but careful socialization is also crucial. A puppy from sound lines, with parents of excellent temperament, may still be overwhelmed in the presence of children if he is not accustomed to them. The key is to make the puppy comfortable around children from a very early age. If the breeder has children, it will give your Jack Russell an ideal start, as he will be used to them from the very beginning of his life.

In all cases, it is important to work on socializing your puppy as soon as he arrives home. Remember: Even if you do not have young children of your own, you are bound to come across them. You may start a family within your dog's lifetime, you may have grandchildren, or maybe friends' or neighbors' children visit your home. Even if you intend to lead a completely child-free existence for the entire length of your Jack Russell's life, it is still crucial to socialize him with children, as he will undoubtedly meet them when you are out walking.

A dog that has little experience with kids is likely to fear them, and, in some dogs, this can manifest itself in fear-aggression where the dog considers it preferable to attack rather than to be attacked. For example, if you are walking your Jack Russell along a path, and a child passes by and stoops down to pick up a toy, your unsocialized Jack Russell may lash out as a result of being threatened. He sees a hand coming from above and heading in his direction, and bites to prevent "attack" from something he considers to be "alien" and unfamiliar. Misunderstandings like this occur every day. We all read the headlines about the family dog who snapped "for no reason" and who "had never done anything like this before." Often the child does something hardly discernible to humans, but that is deemed threatening by the dog.

> **ff The whole family needs to help with training. JJ**

If your dog develops a child-phobia, you must consult a pet psychologist, but treatment of such a sensitive case can be a lengthy process and is not always guaranteed to work. Prevention is the key. Teach your puppy that children are fun, and make sure he grows up to enjoy their company, and, most important of all, to respect them.

Establishing Status

Your puppy must realize that he is at the bottom of the pack in the family, even lower in status than the youngest child. Although one person is usually responsible for training, it is important to involve all members of the household to some extent. This will help your Jack Russell to realize that he should obey everyone in his new family.

Exercise One

Some dogs can be insecure about hands reaching out to touch their neck or head. To make sure your puppy grows up looking forward to an approaching hand, rather than cringing in terror, or even lashing out, practice the following exercise regularly throughout his puppyhood.

- Be certain the puppy is handled frequently by all members of the family. Supervise closely when children are handling him.
- Put a lightweight puppy collar on your Jack Russell for short, supervised periods when he is in a calm and relaxed mood. Praise him and give a treat.
- After a couple of sessions, if the puppy is happy with the collar, place him on your lap or cradle him in your arms, and hold the collar gently for just a few seconds. Then give him a treat and praise him.
- Over the course of several sessions, increase the length of time he enjoys you holding the collar. If he is unhappy for any reason, go back to holding it for only a very brief time.
- When he is happy with his collar being touched, practice reaching over his head to touch it. Immediately after doing so, give him a treat with your other hand. (Giving a treat with the hand that reaches over may

encourage him to snap in anticipation of a treat.)

- Practice frequently, never forgetting to praise and reward when he doesn't react to the approaching hand. If he does snap, yelp sharply as if in pain and ignore him.

Exercise Two

A dominant or insecure dog may become possessive over his toys and food, and, if threatened, will believe he has the right to defend them. He must be taught that, because he is at the bottom of the pack, everyone in the house has the right to take his things away, and that he must accept this.

Of course, the dog must be respected, too, and it isn't kind to take his toys and food away from him, but it is important that the dog is primed for every eventuality. Accidents and misunderstandings can happen—especially in a house with young children—and it is better to be safe than sorry.

- Sit by the puppy while he is eating one of his meals. Every now and then, put some small pieces of his favorite food (usually chicken or cheese) into his bowl.
- Keep practicing, so that he soon looks forward to hands coming into the bowl.
- Occasionally take his bowl away while he eats, pop some chicken in, and then give it back to him.
- After a couple of weeks, gradually withdraw the treats, so that the puppy doesn't always

Dropping treats into the puppy's bowl will ensure that he does not become possessive about his food bowl.

get a treat after you put your hand in his bowl or after you take the bowl away. Make it random so that he still sees it as a rewarding experience. Always praise effusively when giving the bowl back.

- Be certain the entire family practices the above steps with the puppy so that it doesn't get to the stage where he will allow you to take his food, but will snap if anyone else tries it.

Exercise Three

Teaching pups the *gently* command is always useful, especially with Jack Russells that are so enthusiastic that they can sometimes snap in their excitement to receive a treat.

- Offer the puppy a treat, asking him to take it *"Gently."*
- If he jumps up, snaps, or takes it roughly, yelp, and do not give it to him.
- Keep hold of the treat, as, if you take it away altogether, your puppy will be even more eager to take it quickly when it reappears.
- Repeat the command *"Gently,"* only giving the treat when he takes it from your hand very carefully.
- Regularly repeat the exercise until it is second nature to your pup. You can then move on to training the puppy to take treats gently from children.

Bite Inhibition

Developing good bite inhibition is crucial, even in dogs that are happy around children. Russells are excitable little creatures, but a fun game can get out of hand if the dog plays too roughly and tries to bite. A good bite inhibition is therefore very important, so that the dog *never* bites, even when in a state of high excitement.

Start training the puppy to keep his teeth to himself as soon as you get him home. All puppies "mouth," but it is important for your Jack Russell to realize that humans are always out of bounds. If his teeth make contact with your skin, you must make a high-pitched yelp as if it really hurt (when his needle-sharp puppy teeth are through, you won't have to pretend, because it really *will* be painful!). The puppy will stop as soon as you yelp, surprised at the effect his mouthing has. Ignore him for a few moments afterwards, so he knows he has done wrong. Be consistent, making sure that you—and all members of the family—yelp every time mouthing occurs, no matter how softly he does it.

The intention is not to stop your Jack Russell from chewing, as it is natural for a puppy to chew. Rather, he should be taught to chew suitable toys, such as durable rope tugs, and he should always have access to these toys to satisfy his need to gnaw.

> **" Train your children to respect the new puppy. "**

Rules to Remember

Children need as much training as dogs. Even before you bring the puppy home, they should know the following rules.

- A puppy, however small and sweet, is not a toy.
- Let sleeping dogs lie. A puppy needs long periods of sleep, and should be allowed time to rest undisturbed.
- Teach the children not to play with the pup's toys, and to keep their own toys out of the puppy's reach.
- Teasing is never to be tolerated. Pretending to offer a toy or a treat, then taking it away is asking for trouble—especially with a Jack Russell that will not be made a fool of gladly.
- You get back from a dog what you put into him—give him love and respect, and you will get it back tenfold, making a firm friend for life.

CAT COMPANIONS

Jack Russells were bred to hunt, and the instinct to chase is still very strong. As a result, Russells have a terrible reputation for being cat haters. Admittedly, some are. But they are usually those that have not been raised with cats. Those that have been carefully introduced to cats, and that have been well socialized with them, usually live in complete harmony.

Time and care must be taken, however, since Russells and cats are not natural friends. It is in your best interests to find a breeder who has cats, as the puppies will see them as part of the family, and not as toys that squeak when bitten. Your puppy will also learn a considerable amount from the dam, copying her actions. If the dam chases cats, your Jack Russell will grow up thinking that is what dogs do. If she ignores them, your Jack Russell will remember this, and it will have a bearing on how he behaves toward cats in the future.

Introductions

You may find it useful to put the puppy in a crate prior to introducing your cat. The cat can then safely assess the dog—sniffing him and getting used to him—certain that she cannot be attacked. This may help to build up confidence before the formal introductions take place.

When introducing your Jack Russell to a cat, you should all be as calm as possible. Talk in a low, reassuring voice, as you do not want to excite the puppy. Make sure the puppy is restrained, either by holding him or by keeping him on a lead.

- Ask a friend or family member to cuddle the cat in fairly close proximity to the dog. Ignore the puppy when he shows interest in the cat, and praise and reward him when he pays no attention to her.
- Reassure the cat, and do not force her to stay. If she wants to leave the room, allow her to do so, and resume the introduction later on. Allow the cat an escape (such as a high shelf or access upstairs) in case she feels the need to use it.
- Keep the cat as relaxed as possible so that, if she does want to escape, she will walk away rather than run in panic. A running cat may trigger your pup's chase instinct. Hunting

Terriers and cats are not famous for getting along, but if a puppy is raised with a cat, they will usually learn to live in harmony.

small furry animals is second nature to a Jack Russell, and he will consider it an exciting game. It may be difficult to dissuade him from initiating such a "game" in the future.

- When the cat is confident enough, she will approach the dog for a sniff. Although this is a crucial moment, and you may feel apprehensive about how either one will react, it is very important to remain calm; otherwise, both cat and puppy will pick up on your nervousness and will assume there is something to fear.

- The more positive contact your dog and cat have with each other, the more comfortable they will be. Continue to reward the puppy whenever he ignores the cat. Reassure and reward the cat whenever she is in his presence.

- If your puppy oversteps the mark and is too boisterous, the cat is likely to instill some instant respect in him—by hissing and giving a quick swipe across the nose. Jack Russells are very intelligent dogs with very long memories, and it is unlikely the cat will need to reprimand him twice.

- Do not leave the cat and puppy together unsupervised until you are absolutely sure they can be trusted.

- If, despite your best efforts, the cat/puppy relationship is not improving, you may have to call on the services of a professional dog trainer.

Out and About

If raised carefully, most Jack Russells will happily accept the family cat, but unfamiliar

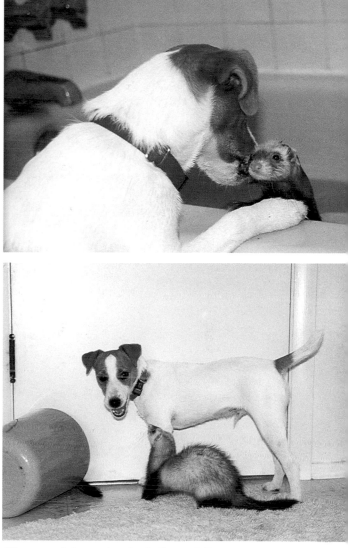

It's very risky to let Jack Russell Terriers play with ferrets.
Photos courtesy: Rani MorningStar.

cats, and other small animals, are a different matter.

It is so natural for your Jack Russell to chase rabbits when out on a walk that it is unlikely you will be able to discourage him from this. Fortunately, most Jack Russells are not fast enough to catch one, but some are. If you find it too upsetting to be brought a "present" on your walks, you will have to work on your dog's *recall* from a very early age (see page 45), so that you can call him back when he is out chasing the local wildlife. Be warned, though: Most Jack Russells become completely focused when hunting a scent or chasing a rabbit, and your dog may be deaf to your calls, despite hours of intensive training.

Meeting the Resident Dog

Introducing your new Jack Russell to an existing dog in the household should be handled sensitively. It is important not to put any noses out of joint, as this will not only affect the dogs' relationship with each other, but may also put at risk their trust in you.

Introducing adult dogs should take place on neutral ground, such as a nearby park, so that the existing dog will not consider the new one to be a threat to his territory. However, because a very young Jack Russell puppy may not have had his vaccinations, you should not risk taking him to an area where adult dogs may have

Allow the resident dog and the puppy to sort out their own relationship.
Photo courtesy: Chris Cox.

exercised. When your puppy is older, let them meet each other in the house or in your backyard. Remove any toys or chews, as these can cause conflict if your existing dog feels threatened and feels he should defend his belongings.

In the majority of cases, the existing dog will assume the status of top dog. Most well-socialized puppies will be more than happy to accept the position of underdog. For this reason, it is important not to allow the puppy to get away with things for which you would reprimand your older dog. If, for example, you do not allow your existing dog to sleep on your bed, it is a grave mistake to let the puppy do so, as both dogs will interpret this as the puppy being elevated to top dog status.

Your existing dog will probably show he is boss by growling if the puppy oversteps the mark. If, for example, the puppy tries to help himself to his elder's food or toys, your dog is likely to show his disapproval. However tempting it may be to intervene, you must resist and leave them to sort out their own positions. Reprimanding the dog for grumbling at the puppy will undermine the dog's position, and will cause confusion.

Of course, if your puppy is being physically bullied by your dog, you should intervene, but it shouldn't get that far. The odd grumble soon establishes who is boss, and, once they both know their positions, they usually live happily ever after. Occasionally, a dominant puppy and a very submissive older dog come to an agreement that the puppy should be top dog.

Reinforce whatever the dogs decide: feed the top dog first, greet him first, and so on.

FIRST LESSONS

House-training

This is the one area of raising a puppy that fills most new owners with dread, but it does not have to be an uphill struggle. All puppies come with an instinctive willingness to keep their "nest" clean, so you will be working with an eager pupil. Jack Russells are very intelligent little dogs, and your puppy will soon realize what is required.

Some breeders advise owners to house-train the puppy on newspaper, but paper-training simply delays the process, as, once he has learned to use the paper, he is then taught *not* to use the paper and to go outside. This can be confusing to the pup. Why not cut out the paper phase and train him to go outside from the start?

- Choose an area outside in the backyard for your dog to use.
- Take him there regularly throughout the day (see below).
- Use the same place each time. The puppy will come to recognize his own scent and know exactly what to do at this location.
- When the puppy relieves himself, praise him enthusiastically and reward him with a treat.

- Never return indoors immediately after your puppy has relieved himself—even if it is wet or cold outside. Jack Russells love being outdoors, and a puppy is likely to keep you waiting if he realizes he will be taken inside immediately after eliminating. Instead, reward him with a game before returning indoors; carry an umbrella and wear a warm coat if necessary.
- If your puppy fails to perform, try again later on, being especially vigilant of his behavior. If he sniffs the ground, and keeps turning in circling movements, take him outside at once.

Accidents Will Happen

If your puppy has an accident, it is not his fault; it is yours. You should be taking your Jack Russell outside frequently, at key points throughout the day, so that he is given many opportunities to relieve himself. An accident means that you have not been sufficiently attentive to his needs.

"Be consistent in the times you take your puppy out."

Your puppy should be taken outside every couple of hours. If this is not enough, and he still has accidents, take him to his spot more frequently. He should also be taken out:

- First thing in the morning.
- After eating.
- After exercise/play.
- Last thing at night.
- Whenever you see him sniffing the ground or making circling movements.

Vigilance is the key to quick and effective house-training.   *Photo courtesy: Rani MorningStar.*

You should never reprimand your Jack Russell if he does have an accident. It is only natural to feel frustrated at finding a mess after routinely taking him outside throughout the day, but shouting or rubbing his nose in it is cruel and counterproductive. Punishing the puppy can severely damage your relationship and erase all the house-training progress you have made together. The puppy will not realize why you are angry. Some owners claim the pup's look of guilt shows he knows exactly what he has done, but this is not true. A so-called "guilty" look is a submissive one, with the pup doing his best to appease an owner who is angry.

If an accident occurs, clean thoroughly with a proprietary cleaner. Puppies have an excellent sense of smell, and ordinary household disinfectants do not erase the scent; they merely mask it, meaning the puppy will be attracted to the same spot in the future. A special biological cleaner will remove all traces of the mishap, meaning even your Jack Russell cannot sniff out the site of his previous accident.

Caught in the Act

If you find your puppy relieving himself, make a startling noise to stop him immediately. You can clap your hands, or drop a bunch of keys—anything to get his attention. Do not shout, as you don't want the puppy to think you are angry with him: If he thinks that his relieving himself displeases you, he may become secretive, preferring to hide behind the sofa to eliminate than doing so in front of you in the yard.

As soon as the noise stops the puppy from relieving himself, take him outside. Praise him when he finishes in his designated area of the yard.

Silence

If your Jack Russell does not relieve himself when taken out, and has accidents indoors, the secret is to be silent. Keep the puppy in a place where you can see him all the time. Watch his body language, and, as soon as you see the tell-tale signs (i.e., sniffing the ground), silently walk over and take him outside. Take him to the chosen spot. Remember to say nothing. If you excitedly say "Let's go outside" and alert his interest, your puppy is likely to concentrate on you, rather than the task at hand. Remaining quiet will let him get on with relieving himself undisturbed.

CRATE TRAINING

Jack Russells like cozy little dens, and most will take to being in a crate quite easily. The crate should be in a quiet part of the house—such as in a corner of the kitchen. It should have comfortable bedding, and some chew toys to keep the puppy amused. You might drape a blanket over the top and three sides, ensuring that he can still look out of the front of the crate. This will make it a little darker and cozier—more burrowlike—and will keep drafts at bay in the winter.

As well as being enjoyed by the pup, crates are often welcomed by the owner, too, and can be a godsend—provided they are used responsibly. They provide a safe place for the

Used correctly, a crate is beneficial to both puppy and owner.

puppy if, for example, you have workmen in and out of the house, or at times when you are unable to supervise him properly.

A crate should never be used as a puppy prison, confining the dog for long periods of time or shutting him away if he has done something wrong. Your puppy should regard his crate as his own little den, somewhere safe and secure, where he can be left undisturbed. For this reason, children should be taught to leave the puppy alone when he is in his crate.

Although the crate is invaluable during puppyhood, it can be useful throughout your dog's life—at shows, at the veterinarian, or providing a place to stay when you are away from home. Indeed, many adult Jack Russells sleep in a crate out of preference.

CAR TRAVEL

The crate can also be used to transport your Jack Russell in the car. There is nothing more dangerous than a small dog running around loose in the car. The dog should be restrained at all times. It is not only distracting for the driver to have a dog out of control in the car; it can, in the event of an accident, be extremely dangerous for passengers. If you do not use a crate to restrain your Jack Russell, then invest in a doggie car harness to keep him strapped safely to the seat.

Most Jack Russells love car travel, but you should not take this for granted. Introduce your puppy to the car, and teach him that it is an enjoyable place to be.

- Place the crate in the car, with his favorite toys and some comfortable bedding.
- Put your puppy in the crate for just a few minutes, praising him and giving him his favorite treat—such as liver, chicken, or cheese.
- Gradually increase the length of time he stays in the crate, remembering to make it an enjoyable experience for him.
- When your puppy is happy being in the crate, start the engine and keep it running for a few moments, still praising and keeping him calm.
- When you feel your puppy is ready, take him for a very short trip. Praise and reward him at the end of the trip. Slowly increase the length of the trips.
- If he is sick, make sure he travels on an empty stomach, and perhaps even ask your veterinarian for a suitable treatment. Do not despair if your puppy vomits with alarming regularity in the car—most outgrow it.

ff Teach your puppy he has nothing to fear in the home. JJ

Warning

Never leave your dog unattended in a car. Even on an overcast day or in a shady spot, cars can become like ovens, and many dogs have died from overheating, simply because of an owner's oversight.

On long trips, or on hot days, make regular stops and always make sure your dog has access to fresh water in the car (nonspillable water bowls are available from most pet shops). Car window shades will also make the journey more comfortable.

SOCIALIZATION

As we have seen (when introducing car travel, cats, and children), it is crucial to socialize your puppy to a whole range of experiences if you want him to grow up to be calm and confident. Generally, Jack Russells are not nervous dogs; they are fearless, plucky, and as curious as a cat. Your Jack Russell is unlikely to become a timid pet that jumps at his own shadow, but it is better to be safe than sorry, so give him a good solid start in life by socializing him thoroughly.

Household Appliances

The principle of acclimating the puppy to noisy household appliances is to show that, not only are they not a threat, but that being around them is actually a rewarding experience. For this example, the washing machine will be used, but the same methods can be used to introduce your Jack Russell to the vacuum cleaner, dishwasher, clothes dryer, hairdryer and so on.

- Sit on the kitchen floor, close to the washing machine, and pet the pup. Have a game with his favorite toy.
- When he is engrossed in the game, switch on the machine and set it on a gentle cycle.
- Show no reaction at all to the noise, just continue playing.

The well-socialized puppy will learn to take all new experiences in his stride.

- The puppy should continue with his game or be only slightly distracted. Engage his attention with a toy, rewarding and praising when he ignores the machine.

- Turn the machine off, and continue with the game. Resume the training session later on, gradually extending the time that the washing machine is left on.

- Allow your puppy an easy exit to another room in case it all gets too much for him. It is counterproductive to force him to stay if he is stressed, and it will only increase his anxiety. Stay in the kitchen, playing with a squeaky toy to encourage him back in. Reward him with treats, a game, and lots of praise when he does venture back in.

- When he is really confident while the machine is running, progress to the ground-shaking spin-dry. If he remains calm when this cycle is in full flow, you know you have succeeded.

Visiting The Veterinarian

Some dogs are fearful of visiting the veterinarian. It doesn't take the brightest dog in the world to realize that veterinary visits usually result in needles being stuck into him, pills being forced down his throat, thermometers being shoved up his behind, or worse.

The problem is often compounded because the dog's owner is usually stressed, worrying about how his pet will react, or fearing potential health problems. Although this is perfectly understandable, you must try your utmost not to let your Jack Russell see your concern. Russells are very tuned in to their owners' moods, and will soon pick up on any bad vibes; if the owner is fretful, the dog will start to panic.

- When you visit the veterinarian, for the puppy to be checked over and to start his course of injections, take along some tasty

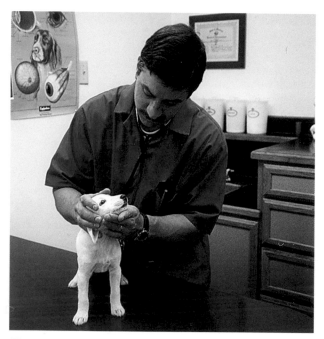

The veterinarian will give your puppy a thorough checkup when he goes to start his vaccinations. Photo courtesy: Rani MorningStar.

treats, and ask the veterinarian to give them to the dog every now and then throughout the consultation. Most will be happy to oblige, knowing that once the dog has made friends, he will be easier to treat in the future.

- Take one of the puppy's blankets to the veterinary clinic and ask if it can be kept in the veterinary clinic, for a week or two. Pop it in the pup's bedding and he will associate the veterinary clinic scent with being warm, content, and comfortable at home.

- Ask if the veterinarian's office organizes puppy/kindergarten parties for those that have been inoculated. Not only are they excellent for socializing the puppy, but they will also show him that veterinary clinics can be fun places, too.

HANDLING TECHNIQUES

To make your Jack Russell a perfect patient, make sure your puppy grows up with no qualms about being examined. This is not simply for your veterinarian's benefit, but will make your life easier, too. You will be able to groom your dog and check him regularly, without it turning into a wrestling match. It is also important if you intend to show your Jack Russell, because show dogs must accept being examined by the judge.

Check Points

- Make sure the puppy is handled by as many different people as possible.
- He should get used to being examined all over—including his belly, tail, and "armpits."
- Check his teeth frequently, and brush them gently with a very soft toothbrush.
- Frequently touch his feet and pads, and check his ears, giving a treat as you do so.
- Check his nails. If they are too long, trim with guillotine-type clippers, making sure you avoid the quick of the nail. If you cut the quick, it will bleed and be painful for the pup, who will be less cooperative about his nails being clipped in the future.
- Groom regularly with a soft brush. Reward your puppy with a treat or two, so he sees it as an enjoyable experience. This will get him used to the routine when his adult coat comes through (see page 64).

The more you do these exercises, the easier they should become, as your puppy will get accustomed to being handled. As long as these

Puppy classes will provide the opportunity of meeting many different breeds, and your pup will learn the canine code of good behavior.

Photo courtesy: Melissa Dailey.

experiences are positive ones, they will strengthen the bond and trust between you.

Puppy Classes

Puppy socialization classes are incredibly important—especially for dominant Jack Russells, that can sometimes grow into little monsters. They may be smaller than many other dogs, but they act as if they are ten times larger, and unless

they are taught from an early age to respect their canine brethren, they may become the local park bullies, detested by all other dog owners.

Okay, so this is the worst-case scenario, but it is better to be safe than sorry. Investing time in your puppy's training will pay dividends in the future.

Puppy classes are great fun for your pup, and, because he will have a whole host of different pals to play with, he will grow up enjoying the

MOTIVATION

When using treats, use only tiny pieces at a time. You don't want to disrupt the flow of training by having your Jack Russell chewing on a treat for several minutes at a time. A tiny amount works just as well in motivating him, giving him enough of a taste to know he wants to earn more. Remember to take the treats out of his daily food allocation so that he does not put on excess weight.

Many Russells prefer toys to treats. Squeaky toys work particularly well, as they love the high-pitched sound (although it will probably drive you crazy after listening to it for hours on end). The terrier's love of squeaks is said to come from its hunting days, when prey would squeal when bitten. Squeak a toy to get your Jack Russell's attention when training, and, as a reward for getting something right, have a quick game with the toy. Be warned though: Some Russells get too excited by the sound of a squeak. Test your own Jack Russell to see whether treats or toys work best.

company of other dogs. Animals teach each other far more than we can ever hope to, and your Jack Russell will learn to speak "doggie language." If he plays too roughly, he will be growled at or bitten back. If he approaches a dog that is not interested in playing, he will be told so in no uncertain terms. If he wants to appease another dog, he will learn how to look submissive. He will learn all this, and much, much more, simply through play.

TRAINING

A Jack Russell needs structure to his life. He also needs to be kept occupied. He is so intelligent that, if he is not mentally stimulated, he will devise his own amusement and turn to "criminal" activities—mugging Great Danes or robbing you of the contents of your refrigerator—instead! Training will make him easier to control and will bring you closer together.

A training class should be a happy place, with dogs being taught using positive, reward-based methods. The old-fashioned methods, of using fear to force the dog to comply with your wishes, are cruel and ruin your relationship with your pet. Sadly, there are still a number of classes that offer this type of training, so look around and ask to observe a class before enrolling.

Teaching your Jack Russell to comply with your wishes, whether it be for him to sit, lie down, or come back, is a way of reinforcing the hierarchical structure in the household, enabling the dog to honor your position. At the same time, training sessions should be enjoyable for both dog and owner—working together, having fun, and building on your relationship with each other.

When a treat is held above his head, your pup will naturally look up and sit.

Sit

Teaching your Jack Russell to sit on command is very useful. You can use it when he is chasing the neighbor's cat, or about to run out onto the road, or for any other situation where you need to stop him in his tracks. It is also useful to make sure he has good manners. Rather than have him jumping up like a pogo stick as you prepare his food, ask him to sit. He can then be rewarded with his meal. If life would be easier without your dog barging ahead through doors and getting under your feet, ask him to sit. You can then walk through, and he can follow behind.

- Hold your pup's favorite treat between your thumb and forefinger.
- Show it to your puppy and, as he attempts to take it, hold it up above his head so that

the only way of him reaching it is by sitting and stretching his neck up.

- Say *"Sit"* and give him the treat as soon as he does so.
- Keep repeating the exercise for short periods, and it won't be long before he will sit on the command alone.
- It also helps the dog to associate the word with the action if you say *"Sit"* whenever you see him sit down throughout the day.

Practice the exercise frequently throughout the day, wherever you are, as repetition is a great learning tool.

Down

"Down" is another useful command. Like *"Sit,"* it should stop the dog in his tracks, but it is more likely to keep him stationary, anchoring him to the spot.

- Put your Jack Russell in the *sit* position.
- Hold a treat in your hand, show it to the pup, and then lower your hand to the floor.
- Make sure you are grasping the treat in your fist, so the dog cannot get to it. The puppy will try every which way he can to get the treat. He will stand up, then stoop down to reach it.
- Eventually, he will realize that the only way to get his head close enough to the hand is to lie down.
- The moment his paws slide forward and his belly touches the floor, say *"Down,"*

Nearly there! A treat is used to encourage the puppy to go into the down position.

give him lots of praise, and make sure you give him the treat he has worked so hard to get.

- Practice regularly throughout each day, and your intelligent Jack Russell will soon be going down when you ask him to.

It may take a little patience, but your puppy will get there in the end.

- Work on associating the command with the activity by saying *"Down"* whenever you see your dog lie down of his own volition.

Stay

A dog that will stay on command will make your life as a pet owner very much easier. It will be helpful in a variety of situations, and can even be a lifesaver. For example, when you open the car to let him out, you can tell him to stay until you have put a lead on him.

- Position the puppy in a *down* and tell him, to *"Stay."*
- Step back, wait for just a few seconds, then call him to you, praise him, and give him a treat.
- If, at any point, you see he is about to move, repeat *"Stay"* sternly.
- Repeat the exercise, eventually increasingly the time he will stay.
- Take the training very slowly. If he consistently stays at 10 seconds, try 15, but do not increase the length of time of the *stay* until he has fully mastered the current stay.
- If he breaks the *stay,* do not reward him with a treat. Return to practicing shorter *stays,* only attempting longer ones when he is absolutely ready.
- When he will stay consistently, take another step back, and repeat the steps above.
- Gradually increase the distance between you, again making sure that you step back only when your Jack Russell has mastered each distance.
- Practice the *stay* command whenever you get the opportunity—and don't forget to make him feel very clever when he gets it right.

Collar and Lead

Being the independent, free-spirited dog he is, your Jack Russell may initially object to wearing a collar, and he may resist walking with you on the lead. However, if both collar and lead are introduced in a positive way, backed up with rewards and praise, your puppy will soon become relaxed and happy.

Exercise One

- Put a soft, lightweight puppy collar on your Jack Russell for short periods at a time. Have some fun with him—give a couple of treats and play a game with a squeaky toy. This should distract him from trying to scratch off the collar.
- Gradually increase the length of time the collar is left on. Remember that he

The body language says it all – "Stay."

should never be left unsupervised when wearing a collar. If it gets caught on something, it can strangle your dog, so only put it on when you are going out lead-walking together.

- Do not attempt to introduce the lead into the equation until your puppy is comfortable wearing a collar.

Exercise Two

Practice the following exercise in the garden, remembering not to venture out into public places until your puppy has had the full course of vaccinations.

A toy can be used to encourage your puppy to walk forward on the lead.

- To teach the puppy to walk in a well-mannered way on a lead, sit him on your left. Attach the lead, and hold it with your right hand.
- In your left hand, hold a treat or a squeaky toy.
- Walk forward slowly. When he walks beside you, say *"Heel,"* praise him, and give him a treat to encourage him to go forward.
- If your puppy surges ahead, pulling on the lead, stop at once. He must learn that if he pulls on the lead, he gets nowhere fast. Call him back, sit him beside you and try again.
- If he becomes distracted by other dogs or people walking past, remind him to *"Heel,"* and occasionally squeak the toy to get him focused on you again.
- When he gets the hang of walking beside you, introduce some variations. Turn left or right, walk in a circle, or suddenly stop. This will also stop him from becoming complacent, and will encourage him to concentrate.

Recall or Come

Most puppies ignore their owners when there are more interesting things to do and see, but the Jack Russell is particularly prone to selective hearing. The moment he catches an interesting scent to follow, you can call all you like, but he will not respond until he has finished his own business.

Many owners make the mistake of not teaching the *recall* or *come* at an early stage, as it is relatively easy to catch a puppy. However, this backfires as soon as the dog gets older, becomes more independent, and his sense of smell becomes more acute. Therefore, it is well worth investing the time in teaching a good response to the *recall* or *come* before major problems develop.

Exercise One

- Make sure the pup is familiar with his name. Repeat it frequently when talking to him or petting him.
- Ask your puppy to *"Sit"* and to *"Wait,"* and kneel a little distance from him. Say his name and ask him to *"Come."* Show him you really want him to be with you. Use an excited tone of voice, pat your legs or clap your hands, squeak a toy, show him a treat, anything to tempt him to come.
- Make a big fuss when he does come, and reward him with a treat or a game.
- Gradually increase the distance your puppy has to come to you. Call him from the kitchen when he is in the living room and, if you want to gauge whether you have really succeeded, call him from his food.

Exercise Two

When your puppy has had his vaccinations, and he will reliably come to you indoors and in your garden, you can practice in a park, where there are likely to be many more distractions.

- Put him on a line (an extra-long lead).
- Ask him to *"Sit"* and *"Wait,"* and walk a little distance away from him.
- Call his name and ask him to *"Come."* As before, encourage him to come by using a treat or a toy. Reward him when he does so.
- Every time he comes when called, praise him and extend the line so he is further away. If he does not respond to your call, shorten the line until he does come. Then gradually extend the length as he masters each distance.
- When you are confident that he will always come when called, remove the line and practice without it.

The recall *is* probably the most important exercise to teach your Jack Russell.

Exercise should be limited during the vulnerable growing period.

- On a walk, call your dog back regularly, praise and pet him, then send him off to continue playing. Never put him on the lead immediately after calling him back. Coming to you should be a rewarding experience; if it spells the end of an exciting walk, he will be reluctant to come back.

For adolescent recall problems, see page 53.

EXERCISE

Exercising your Jack Russell is one of the joys of dog ownership—but care must be taken during the vulnerable stage when your puppy is growing. All too often, a puppy ends up with an injury caused by boisterous play or by jumping off furniture.

It is important to supervise your puppy so that he does not leap on and off the furniture. Access to stairs must also be restricted until he reaches about six months, when his bones should be stronger. If you do not have a door that restricts access to the stairs, a child stair-gate is a worthwhile investment.

Build up exercise gradually, so that your Jack Russell does not overstrain himself. Prior to the vaccination course being completed, your puppy will get sufficient exercise playing in the garden. Following vaccinations, you can take your puppy out for a 10-minute session on the lead each day. Make sure you walk on hard surfaces, as well as soft ones, as this will help keep his nails trimmed.

Each puppy is different. Monitor and respond to your pup's needs. Some need more exercise than others and will drive you crazy, racing around the living room to use up excess energy. Others are more sedentary and will take life at a steadier pace. Remember that three or four short walks a day are preferable to one long hike. They will break up the day for the puppy, and will not wear him out or damage his growing bones.

An adult Jack Russell will need free-running exercise, but a run around the yard is enough for a puppy—especially if you play with him, giving mental as well as physical exercise.

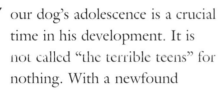

CHAPTER FOUR

THE ADOLESCENT JACK RUSSELL

Your dog's adolescence is a crucial time in his development. It is not called "the terrible teens" for nothing. With a newfound confidence and hormones running through his veins, your Jack Russell is likely to test your patience to its limits. But, as with human teenagers, most dogs soon grow out of it, so be firm but fair, and just hang in there.

LEADERSHIP

Your dog will start reaching sexual maturity around six months of age, though it varies from dog to dog. Not only does the dog change physically, losing his roly-poly puppy shape and taking on the shape of an adult Jack Russell, he can also experience behavioral changes.

He is likely to be quite puppyish still, but will start to display some adult behavior. In the case of a male, this could manifest itself in behavior such as leg-humping, where he mounts anything available, such as legs or cushions. It is a mistake to let him mount—and, worse still, to laugh at

his actions. Jack Russells are natural clowns and love being the center of attention; if he thinks leg-humping pleases his "audience," he may continue to do it, even if his sexual urges have been removed by neutering. The moment you see your Jack Russell mounting, tell him to *"Leave it,"* and immediately distract him with an alternative activity.

This no-man's-land between puppyhood and adulthood can be very confusing for your Jack Russell. Being the quick-thinking opportunists they are, Jack Russells can spot a weakness as easily as they can a spot a rabbit, and are often quick to exploit any lapse in leadership. During this time, he will need you to be a strong and assertive leader. If you give him an inch, he will take a mile, so be consistent in your discipline, and do not allow him to get away with something that you would normally not tolerate. If you put in the hard work for the dog's first year, you will find it much easier later on. The dog will know the rules, and will stop trying to break them.

RALEY OFF THE RAILS

Helen Noble had always wanted a Jack Russell. Having worked with horses, where Russells were always around the yard, Helen had some experience caring for the breed—or so she thought.

"I bought, Raley, my first Jack Russell, in March. My boyfriend had Labrador Retrievers, but Raley was my first dog, so it was quite a baptism of fire.

"Raley will be nine months old this week, and he is very one-track-minded. When he finds something he wants, you can call him a thousand times and he won't come. He has just discovered rabbit scents, and won't be budged from them.

"Raley's very protective of his family. We take him boating, and he watches us all. If I get out of the boat to water ski, he becomes unsettled and won't relax again until I am back in. He likes everyone to be where he can see them. He's not so fussy about staying where *we* can see *him*, though! He has escaped three times. We have a four-foot fence, and he leaps up and then climbs the rest!

"In some respects, Raley is better behaved than other dogs. My boss got a puppy at the same time as I, and his Jack Russell was digging holes everywhere and chewing everything. Raley doesn't dig and he only chews his toys. He is the same age as the other dog, but is much more mature—he isn't so puppyish.

"We don't have any trouble with Raley being aggressive to other dogs. I knew that Russells could be troublesome if they were not socialized, so, as soon as Raley had his shots, I made sure he met as many dogs as possible. He is very subservient, and loves playing. He will crawl on his belly to another dog, tail wagging, as if to say, 'I'm a friend; please play with me.'

"But smaller animals are a different matter. We have friends who own gerbils. As soon as Raley saw them, that was it: He stood there with his nose to the cage and his tail wagging. He would not be distracted, and we could not call him away—he was focused on the gerbils. We had to physically remove him from them.

On board, Raley keeps a close eye on proceedings. Photo courtesy: Helen Noble.

"Raley loves to play. He has a rope tug-toy that he takes all his pent-up energy out on. If anyone saw us play with him, they would think he was violent, but he's not. He's got very good bite inhibition now. When he was 16 weeks old, he started snapping at us, but we would give a sharp yell and tap him on the nose. He suddenly saw that we could discipline him, and seemed to say 'Okay, you're the leader.' He hasn't bitten us since."

PROBLEM BEHAVIOR

Car Alarm

Jack Russells are prone to the possessive guarding of "their" car. This can take the form of head-butting the window every time someone or something passes by the car, leaping up and down, or barking like something possessed. Do not con yourself into thinking your pet will be a good deterrent against would-be thieves. This behavior is dangerous—and in any case, dogs should never be left unattended in cars (see page 37).

- If your Jack Russell is a motor maniac, train him to enjoy the crate (see page 37).
- Once he is happy sitting in the crate, and is rewarded with his favorite treats for being calm in it, then you should enlist the help of willing friends to walk past the car, while you keep him occupied with a squeaky toy or treats.
- Ignore him and withhold the rewards if he barks at a volunteer. Return to the training, and pay him attention, only when he is quiet.
- When he is consistently quiet and comfortable with someone passing by, gradually withdraw the treats, giving them only randomly. Use verbal praise instead.
- Start taking him on short car trips, praising him when he is quiet and well-behaved.
- Ignore him when he is noisy. Yelling at him to be quiet will only worsen the situation. Your Jack Russell will believe

you are "barking," because you also perceive the passer by to be a threat. He will then become increasingly agitated and will bark louder and more furiously to drive the threat away.

Mailboxes

You rarely have to persuade a Jack Russell to become a watchdog. Most are so nosy they will find a good vantage point by a window, and tell you if someone is at the door or passes by the house. It can provide a sense of security to have a burglar deterrent in the house, but it can also be a complete nuisance if your Jack Russell starts perceiving a threat in the most innocent of events—such as the mailman delivering letters.

The best thing is to preempt the behavior by getting a new pup to associate the mail delivery with another activity or reward. Having a treat or a game will encourage him to see the mailman's arrival as a positive experience and should stop him trying to chase him away. If

The watchful Jack Russell can become over-enthusiastic in his duties.
Photo courtesy: Melissa Dailey.

your dog shows signs of developing problem behavior, it may also be useful to remove any vantage points (chairs by the window, etc.) to limit any obsessive territorial guarding.

It may be amusing to see a Jack Russell bounce up and down at the mailbox, but it is not so funny for the mailman who fears he will be bitten every morning—nor is it quite so endearing when important letters and invaluable documents are chewed up.

ff Focus your Jack Russell's attention with mouth-watering treats. ff

The reason why a Jack Russell "attacks" the mail is a perfectly logical one: An "intruder" approaches the house and attempts to get near the front door, but is scared away by barking, growling, and snapping. He leaves behind some "foreign" material with an unfamiliar scent, and launches another intrusion the next day... and the next... and the next... .

It will be very difficult to discourage your Jack Russell from this behavior as, in his eyes, he is defending his house, and his aggression has the desired effect: Every day, he scares the would-be intruder away.

Your reaction to your terrier's behavior may make it worse, and create a vicious circle that is difficult to break. For example, yelling at the dog when he attacks the mailbox will make him believe you too are shouting at the mailman, encouraging him to defend his territory all the more vigilantly. You will probably start to dread the mail delivery, and will act nervously in anticipation of your Jack Russell's reaction. Your dog will sense this, and become even more agitated.

The first step should be to crate your Jack Russell at the regular mail time. If your Jack Russell is prevented access to the mailbox, your mail will be safe, as will your mailman's fingers.

Now you must turn your attention to solving the problem. The key is to remain calm and to ignore your eager watchdog's guarding completely. Ideally, you want to distract him from racing to the door and barking, but it will be a hard habit to break, as it is likely to have become part of his daily routine. About five minutes before your mailman is due to arrive, take your Jack Russell out to the yard and play a game with his favorite toys. Make sure he is completely distracted during the mailman's visit.

Continue this for about a week to break the former routine. Then move indoors to play a game in a room at the back of the house, away from the front door. If your Jack Russell hears the mail, and barks, turn away from him and stop the game. Do not have any eye contact with him. Only resume the game when he has been quiet. Remember not to play just any old game—it has to be really fun and exciting—far more entertaining than his favorite game of chasing the mailman away.

When you are able to distract him successfully, move to the front room, closest to the mailbox, and repeat the procedure. When he is ignoring the mail from this room, sit with him just a few minutes before the mailman arrives until after he leaves. Give him treats—something very special—to keep him focused on you. Give them to him when he is quiet, and withdraw them if he is noisy. Praise and pet him when he is silent to show him that this behavior pleases you.

Stick with it, and your hard work should pay off. If not, seek the advice of a professional dog trainer or psychologist.

Recall

Recall or *come* can be a real problem when your Jack Russell hits canine adolescence. With so many fascinating smells, and interesting things to investigate, many Russells become deaf to their owners' desperate pleas to return.

I have heard of one owner who spent hours calling and searching for her dog that had just disappeared in the woods. She remembered the advice of a forest ranger, that you should leave your coat in the area where your dog was last spotted. She did so, after she could search no more, and, when she came back, her errant Jack Russell was lying on the coat fast asleep.

Hopefully, you will not have to resort to such extreme action. Leaving a dog loose could easily end in heartbreak—especially if he runs into the street. It will save you considerable worry if you prevent *recall* from becoming a problem, before it escalates to such a degree.

Work on your pup's *recall* when he is still a young pup (see exercises in Chapter Three), and keep on top of his *recall* by practicing the exercises throughout his adulthood. The most important thing to remember is that you must remain very exciting to your dog. Even at 6 A.M., on a cold, wet, windy day, you must exude enthusiasm and be a fun person to be with.

A beguiling scent, or something interesting on the horizon—and your Jack Russell instantly "forgets" his recall lessons.

Jack Russells are clever little dogs, and it does not take them long to realize that most owners call them back only when they want to put the lead on and go home. Refusing to come therefore prolongs their walk.

Carry treats in your pocket, and call your dog back throughout the walk to give them to him. A high-pitched squeaky toy is also a good bargaining tool. Squeak it to call your Jack Russell over to you, and then have a game with the toy. He will soon realize that is it worth his while to come when called, as it results in a reward, and doesn't necessarily signal the end of a walk. It may be worth feeding him on his walk. Hunger will encourage him to come back to you.

Acting unpredictably also keeps dogs on their toes. Most wander off, knowing their reliable owner will be where they left them. Your Jack Russell must learn not to take you for granted. When walking with your dog, turn around and walk or run the other way, hide behind a tree, just to make him realize he has to keep an eye on what you are doing, and to stay close.

If, despite your best efforts, your Jack Russell's instincts to hunt are too strong, and *recall* is a real problem, take him out only on a long training line—and seek the advice of a professional trainer or behaviorist.

Aggression

Despite their yappy-snappy reputation, Jack Russells from good parentage that have been raised and socialized in the right environment should show no aggression. As working dogs, they had to get along not only with each other, but also with their handler. A dog that

snapped at his owner was of no use at all, nor was one who preferred bickering with his coworkers rather than working as a team on a hunt. A dog with undesirable aggressive traits would have been euthanized pretty quickly, and would not have been used for breeding, ensuring that the amenable temperament of the breed was kept pure.

Unfortunately, the popularity of the Jack Russell has led to some indiscriminate breeding, producing a number of dogs with an atypical temperament, which gives the rest of the breed a bad name.

If your Jack Russell shows any aggression, particularly toward people, you must seek immediate professional advice from a dog trainer. Aggression—even in a small breed—is a very serious problem and could result in someone being hurt and your dog being destroyed. Above all, you must never react to aggression with aggression, as it will only aggravate the problem. Aggression can only get worse, so do not delay in seeking professional help at the first sign of a problem.

SPAYING AND NEUTERING

Bad behavior is not always caused by hormones. It is simpler for an owner to think that their dog has become an innocent victim of testosterone, but often bad behavior is the result of bad handling (see Leadership, page 49). However, spaying or neutering is always an option if your veterinarian thinks that hormones are responsible for your Jack Russell's hooliganism.

Jack Russells should get along well with each other, and with their handler, showing no signs of aggression.

If you do not plan to breed your Jack Russell, give careful thought to the option of spaying or neutering. Photo courtesy: Melissa Dailey.

Spaying or neutering is a good idea if you do not plan to show or breed your male or female. Spaying or neutering has many health benefits. Removing the womb in a bitch removes the chance of her developing pyometra, a potentially life-threatening condition in which the womb fills with pus. Mammary tumors are also less likely to occur. Prostate disorders are reduced in male dogs that have been neutered.

Some owners have found a bitch is more prone to gaining weight once spayed, but a controlled diet will solve this problem. Occasional incontinence when the bitch is older is also sometimes cited as a disadvantage, but some unneutered older bitches can become incontinent too.

Many veterinarians now are neutering cats and dogs as early as 12 weeks of age. Some still prefer to wait until the dog reaches sexual maturity and until after the bitch has had her first season. If you don't want your male dog to develop some very masculine behaviors (such as marking everything in sight—and smell), early neutering can be more effective than waiting until sexual maturity; some behaviors have by then become habitual, rather than merely hormonal.

Talk to your veterinarian about what he or she would advise for your Jack Russell and when the best time would be to have the dog neutered.

CHAPTER FIVE

THE FAMILY DOG

ull of fun and energy, the Jack Russell lives life in the fast lane and you will soon find there are no dull moments when a Jack Russell is around. It is your job to channel these natural high spirits so you and your family enjoy the companionship of a lively, but controllable dog.

HOME LIFE

A Jack Russell thrives in a family environment, enjoying the comings and goings of his human "pack," and being stimulated by the hustle and bustle of daily life. He is a notoriously "nosy neighbor," and will probably spend much of his time peering out of a window to see what everyone is up to, warning you if anyone approaches the house. By the evening—provided he has been given ample exercise during the day—your pet will be happy to spend quiet evenings curled up with his family.

In many ways, the playful Jack Russell is an ideal companion for children to grow up with. But do not take the relationship for granted. This is a breed that needs firm handling and control so that he respects authority. Make sure the child/dog relationship gets off to a good start by working on the exercises outlined in Chapter Three.

A Jack Russell loves to be included in family outings, but there are times when he has to be home alone. Do not leave your Jack Russell alone for longer than is necessary, and make sure he is kept occupied with safe toys to chew on. A bored Jack Russell is a troublemaking Jack Russell, and he will undoubtedly find trouble if left to his own devices.

A puppy accustomed to being left alone for short periods from an early age will be quite content to be on his own, awaiting your return. Separation anxiety, when a dog becomes highly distressed and often destructive if he is left alone, is usually the result of an owner failing to familiarize the puppy with this routine.

TWO KIDS AND A DOG

Diane Cain thought her family was incomplete without a dog, so she took on Abbey, a Jack Russell pup.

"I wanted a dog that could live indoors, was low maintenance (no expensive professional dog grooming every month), was healthy, playful, good around kids, smart, and could travel. I did a little reading, and fell in love with the Jack Russell.

"We bought the pup when my oldest daughter, Cassi, was seven years old. She had been begging for a puppy for a long time; she was eager to take on responsibility and care for the pup—and she is learning fast.

"Reflecting back on my own childhood, I had an Irish Setter, a German Shorthaired Pointer, gerbils, guinea pigs, fish, a parakeet, a cat, and a couple of horses. My passion was horses. I had to trudge through the snow in the winter every day to feed the horses in the morning before I went to school, to groom and exercise them, and to make sure their water was full and didn't turn to ice, every day. I was a teenager at the time, and loved horses so much that no matter what the weather was, I was willing to endure the tasks of keeping them—my point being, whether the pet is a dog, fish, or a horse, as a child, the responsibility that I had for that pet was mine, and if I chose not to keep it up, I would lose my friend.

Abbey helped teach the children a sense of responsibility.
Photo courtesy: Diane Cain.

"I think, for children growing up, a pet is one of life's necessary steps in their growth.

"My daughter gets up every morning and lets our Jack Russell, Abbey, out of her crate, feeds her, and then plays with her until she has to go to school.

"As a puppy, Abbey was very energetic. At first, she would run after Cassi. Biting ankles and jumping up was all fun and games—until those sharp little puppy teeth scraped the skin. So we devised new rules:

1. If Abbey starts biting at your ankles you say *'No'* and give her something else to chew on.
2. If she chews on anything that's not hers, you say *'No'* and give her one of her toys.
3. Abbey should always sleep in the crate, no exceptions.
4. When you leave the house, Abbey goes into the crate.
5. Abbey must be in a crate if traveling, no exceptions.

"The crate is not for punishment, but for security. It's Abbey's bedroom. So if we go somewhere to visit, we take her in the crate, and she will feel comfortable in the strange surroundings because she has her bedroom with her.

"This breed is very smart, but needs total discipline—like a child. They know what *'No'* means, so you make the rules, or they will rule you!"

DIRTY HARRI

No one is exactly sure of Harri's history. Abandoned as a puppy, the two-year-old Jack Russell spent the first 18 months of his life living on a trash heap, scavenging for enough food to survive each day. He was thin, dirty, and had a broken leg, yet he managed to avoid being rescued by concerned staff members of the National Canine Defense League in the United Kingdom. Eventually, sanitation workers were successful in capturing Harri, and he was taken into the animal shelter, where he received lots of love and medical attention. Sadly, Harri's leg could not be saved, and had to be amputated, but that has not slowed him down, as his new owner, Debra Confrey, explains.

"Harri had been living wild on the heap for so long, and was very nervous around people. The sanitation workers would throw food to him, but he wouldn't let anyone near him. He can still be a little afraid of people—especially big men. Yet, when he was taken in to the National Canine Defense League, he surprised everyone by his enthusiasm for life, and seemed to want nothing more than kisses and cuddles from everyone he met.

"When my husband agreed we could have a dog, we visited the animal shelter. Harri was the second dog we came to. He came up, wagging his tail, and I fell in love with his cheeky grin. It wasn't until he bounced away that I realized he had three legs.

"Harri had been at the center for four months. A lot of people had asked about Harri as he had been featured in the newspapers, but most seemed to have been frightened off by his amputated leg, perhaps thinking it would be difficult to cope with.

"Harri was not house-trained when we took him in, but, within two days at home he understood what was required—and he hasn't had an accident since.

"For the first few months after Harri arrived, I had to be very careful and keep him on the lead whenever we went out, as the National Canine Defense League was worried that Harri's instinct might be to run away. To help us learn how to work together and trust each other, we enrolled in an Obedience class, and, although it was hard work, at the end of it Harri and I had learned some valuable lessons.

"Another very important part of our training was getting Harri used to his new life, and from his first day at home, Harri came everywhere with me to get him socialized to as many new experiences as possible.

Abandoned as a puppy, Harri has now found a loving home.
Photo courtesy: Debra Confrey.

"The final problem we had to tackle was Harri's weight and general health. A combination of 18 months fending for himself, followed by the amputation of his leg, and then three months in kennels awaiting a new home, had left Harri very thin.

"At first, I had to sit with him to encourage him to eat, but after a few weeks he began to put on weight and muscle, and his general health and condition improved enormously.

"Harri has made a fantastic recovery. My most satisfying moment with Harri was the first time I watched him push back his ears, feel the wind on his face, and run around the park, without any fear of ever being lost or frightened again."

CARING FOR THE ADULT DOG

Feeding

Jack Russells are not fussy eaters, so you should not have a problem finding a food that your dog enjoys. It is important to remember that your dog's age and lifestyle will affect his nutritional needs. An active, working youngster will need a different diet than an elderly, sedentary dog. If you breed your female, she will need many more calories than usual when she is feeding her puppies. Many complete food brands cater to the dog's changing needs from puppyhood on.

Complete diets take the hassle out of feeding your dog, but it is a matter of personal choice whether you prefer the traditional dry food or canned menu. If there is any doubt about your Jack Russell's diet, talk to your Jack Russell's breeder or your veterinarian.

Obesity can be a problem in the breed, so make sure you feed according to your dog's age and size, and the amount of exercise he gets.

Weight

There are so many different sizes of Jack Russell—from the short bow-legged dogs to the taller purebred dogs—that it is impossible to give a definitive ideal weight. Traditionally, the male Jack Russell was 14 inches (36 cm) and 14 pounds (6 kg), but that does not account for heavier-boned dogs, or the shorter dogs. A general rule of thumb is that the dog should be one pound per inch with one pound on top.

Obesity is a very serious problem: It not only reduces the dog's quality of life; it may actually shorten it. Do not kill your dog with kindness by overfeeding, or by spoiling him with too many treats. If your dog is overweight, contact your veterinarian. Most clinics now have weight classes that your dog can attend.

Exercise

Russells love the outdoors and a good walk is the highlight of their day. Generally, a Jack Russell needs about two half-hour periods of walks daily. Some need more; some need less. Gauge how much your dog needs and adjust his exercise accordingly. Remember not to wear him out too much. Being such a stubborn creature, the Jack Russell will rarely give in, and will go all day before admitting that he is worn out.

Some people say that the Jack Russell was born a country dog and that he should remain one—that it is cruel to keep him in a town environment. However, in most towns there are more opportunities to exercise a dog than in many parts of the countryside, where much of the land belongs to farms. As long as your Jack

EXERCISING YOUR JACK RUSSELL
The adaptable Jack Russell will enjoy the exercise he is given—in whatever form it takes.

Photo courtesy: Cynthia Bliven.

Photo courtesy: Diana Eaton.

Photo courtesy: Sue Porter.

Photo courtesy: Rani MorningStar.

Photo courtesy: Mary Strom.

Russell can get a good walk in a safe environment, he will be happy wherever he is.

Allowing your terrier access to a fenced yard where he can play in between his walks is also important. A game of tug (not too strenuous or it can ruin his teeth), or playing with a squeaky toy will be a source of great enjoyment.

The natural instinct of a Jack Russell is to dig—and you must be aware of this if your dog lives in a suburban area. Your dog's aptitude for digging will also leave its mark in your yard.

The fence foundations should be well into the ground, with no gaps, to make sure your Jack Russell cannot dig to freedom. If you want to keep your yard intact, it is advisable to provide a place where he *can* excavate to his heart's content. Encourage and reward your Jack Russell when he digs in the allocated area, and give a stern *"No"* when he ventures elsewhere.

Remember that, as well as going under, your Jack Russell is also very good at going over—leaping and climbing—so make sure you have a fence that is at least 6 feet (1.8 m) high that can withstand the famous Jack Russell bounce.

GROOMING

A Jack Russell does not require extensive grooming care. Unlike many of the smaller breeds, his coat is not there to make him look pretty; it is there simply to protect him when he is working. However, it will need some attention to keep it in good condition.

Bred to dig, your Jack Russell will inevitably end up looking like this.

Bathing

Russells enjoy getting dirty. They will think nothing of shooting down a muddy hole and coming back up looking like a swamp monster. Fortunately, the terrier coat is designed for such abuse, and once dry, dirt usually brushes off easily.

Bathing too frequently creates a soft coat, which is undesirable in a Jack Russell. However, sometimes there is no getting away from the fact that your dirty terrier needs a bath. Some hate water, others love it, but, if you have acclimated your dog to bath time being an enjoyable experience from an early age (treats help!), then it need not turn into an unpleasant wrestling match.

Being a small breed, Jack Russells can easily fit into a sink, rather than a bathtub where you have to stoop over the dog. Use a bath mat in the bottom of the sink, to prevent the dog from sliding around. Wet the coat, leaving the head until last (many dogs dislike having their head wet, so wet it gently). Use a good dog shampoo, and create a lather. Rinse through thoroughly. In some cases, a second shampoo and rinse may be necessary.

Towel-dry the dog thoroughly. You can use a hairdryer on a moderate heat to speed up the process.

Brushing

Brush through the coat with a slicker brush (fine wire-toothed brush) at least once a week to remove any loose hair. When your dog is shedding, you should brush him daily. Brush

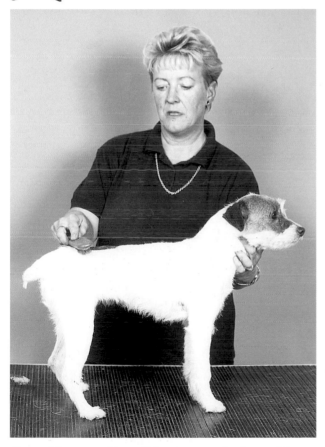

A weekly grooming will keep your dog's coat in good shape, and it also provides the opportunity to give him a once-over.

the entire dog, not forgetting the belly and under the arms. Remember that the thick undercoat should be brushed, as well as the topcoat, so do not just brush the surface, but go right through both coats.

Once there are no tangles, use the narrow-toothed part of a comb to remove the last stray loose hairs.

Stripping

Rough-coated or broken-coated terriers need to be "hand-stripped." This involves removing the loose hairs in the topcoat by plucking them out. It should be completely painless to the dog, provided the dog is shedding at the time, and that you are only gently pulling out those hairs that are already loose. If the hair is not coming out easily, then the coat is not ready, and you should wait another couple of weeks before trying again.

Stripping is usually done in the spring, when the dog starts shedding, but some dogs may need it to be done more frequently. It takes about two months for the new coat to come through after stripping.

Before you start stripping, take a step back to look at your dog to see where particular attention is needed. Some Jack Russells, for example, do not need very much attention paid to the hair under the eyes.

- Brush and comb thoroughly, both against and along the natural lie of the coat.
- Apply grooming chalk to the coat, making it easier to grip, and comb the hair up.

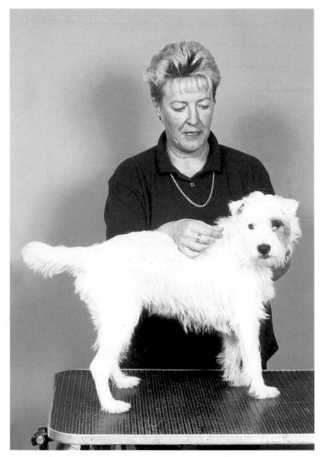

Stripping is done by plucking the hair between the finger and thumb. It is completely painless.

- Take the hair between your thumb and forefinger (or between your thumb and stripping knife) and pull it down.
- Work around the body, stripping the entire coat on the body, and neaten up the tail, knees, feet, elbows, and face.
- Tidy up the face and feet with a small slicker brush.
- Trim carefully around the feet, and, with the male, around the genitals.
- Give a final brush-through to remove any stray hairs.

- Some owners have found that bathing the coat in an antibacterial shampoo helps to soothe any irritation to the skin after stripping.

If you do not show your dog, you might prefer to control his coat growth by taking him to a groomer to be clipped, rather than hand-stripping.

ROUTINE CARE

General Checks

Your Jack Russell is more than likely to come home from a walk covered in burrs and seeds, so check him over at the end of your outing. Pay particular attention to his feet, as grass seeds can work their way deep into a pad if left. Jack Russells dive head first into most situations (literally as well as metaphorically), so the eyes can have a buildup of debris. Clean gently with a moist tissue or cotton.

You should also regularly check your Jack Russell for any signs of parasites, such as fleas and ticks, and treat accordingly (see Chapter Nine).

Ears

You should regularly clean your Jack Russell's ears with a proprietary ear cleaner, and should check for any sign of mites. If your terrier keeps shaking or pawing at his ears, or if the ears have a bad smell, you should consult your veterinarian.

Nails may need trimming if they are not worn down naturally.

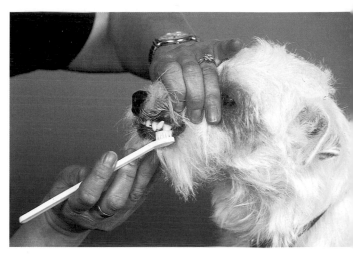

Regular cleaning will guard against tooth decay and gum disease.

Nails

Your Jack Russell's nails should be kept trimmed. A dog that leads an active life, and that is exercised on pavements as well as on grass, usually wears the nails down naturally, but it is worth keeping an eye on them, particularly if you have an older dog.

Guillotine-type nail clippers should be used to trim the ends of the nails. You must be careful to avoid the quick (dark vein) in the nail as it will bleed and cause pain to your terrier if it is nicked.

Dental Care

Teeth should be cleaned regularly to avoid bad breath and tooth decay. This is especially important to prevent your Jack Russell from developing dental problems when he is older. A clean, fresh mouth will improve your dog's quality of life.

Use a toothbrush or a fingerbrush to clean the teeth. Special toothpaste for dogs is available, and will probably persuade your terrier that teeth cleaning isn't such an ordeal after all.

GOLDEN OLDIES

Jack Russells remain puppyish and young at heart for most of their lives. As far as a Jack Russell is concerned, there is no such thing as middle age—there is puppyhood and old age. And even in the autumn of his life, most Russells insist on growing old disgracefully.

Although your Jack Russell may refuse to accept he is getting older, this does not mean you should ignore his changing needs. The older Jack Russell is likely to need less exercise and food, and more warmth. He will be reluctant to eat less—and certainly to exercise less—so it is your responsibility to make sure he doesn't overdo it.

Do not neglect his routine care. His teeth, particularly, will need regular attention, and it is important to watch for any lumps or bumps, and any change in behavior, such as increased

Make the older dog feel special, and try to respond to his changing needs.

thirst. Contact your veterinarian if you have any concerns.

As well as caring for his physical needs, it is important also to accommodate your Jack Russell's changing emotional needs. He may be a little less patient around other dogs, and will tell them in no uncertain terms when he wants to be left alone. He is also likely to become a little more "clingy," wanting more cuddles on a warm lap.

Euthanasia

As a pet owner, it is your responsibility to care for your Jack Russell's well-being, and that includes assuring he does not suffer unnecessarily. If your Jack Russell becomes seriously ill, and the veterinarian advises that no further treatment can be given, it is kinder to put an end to the dog's pain and to let him die in dignity than to have him suffer because

Di Collis had many happy years with her Jack Russell called Bullet, a dog that refused to grow up.

"I had Bullet from when he was a puppy, and, until the age of nine years, he didn't age at all," says Collis. "Then he just got a little slower.

"When I took him out with the younger dogs, Bullet did his utmost to keep up with them. It upset him when he couldn't manage it, so I stopped taking him and the youngsters off-lead together. Terriers just tend to go on and on, and age catches up with them before the body does.

"I had to treat him the same as my other dogs; otherwise, he became very resentful about being treated differently, but I had to make sure he didn't overdo it. My husband used to take Bullet out walking, and, when Bullet got older, he got very distressed when he wasn't taken out. Jack Russells are such go-getters, they won't give in; they'd rather kill themselves than say they have had enough. That is why it is so important to do everything in moderation."

Bullet welcoming newcomer, Ripple.   **Photo courtesy: Di Collis.**

you cannot face letting go. When you have developed a close bond with your Jack Russell through years of sharing your life with him, euthanasia can be a very difficult decision to make. Coping with that loss is also hard. With single-dog households, it can be even harder—in addition to the loss of the companionship, the entire daily routine will also change.

If you have other Jack Russells, you may find that they are also affected by the loss. Russells are very loyal dogs and have been known to grieve when a dog leaves the pack. Your dog may lose his appetite and become withdrawn. If these symptoms continue, you should consult a veterinarian. Similarly, if you find the loss particularly difficult to come to terms with, you should contact a bereavement counselor.

A HEARTBREAKING DECISION

As an experienced veterinary technician, Laurel Pierson has euthanized many animals, but losing her own Jack Russell, Tess, soon after losing her husband, was a very hard blow. "We owned a sweet little female Russell we named Tess," says Laurel. "We had her for about 12 years and during that time, she gave us so much love and enjoyment. She had to be euthanized due to liver failure four years ago.

"When she was about four, she disappeared for two days. When she made her way back home to us, she had been shot in the shoulder with a 22 caliber. bullet and had been poisoned with arsenic. She had such an amazing will to live that she pulled through it all. The arsenic poisoning contributed to her liver failure that ended her life. We never found out who did those horrible things to Tess. She also carried that bullet until the day she died.

"My husband passed away five years ago and Tess was the bright spot in his life. He was only 49 when he died of diabetes. He was terribly ill the last two years of his life. Tess was there for him as his companion, nurse, and retriever. She never left his side for more than a few minutes. That is why it was especially hard to lose her. She was one of the last links I had to him. I take comfort knowing they are together now in a better place.

"I have many years of veterinary experience and have euthanized many dogs and cats myself. It is never an easy task. Sometimes it's much, much harder, especially when the animal is young and healthy. It can also be a blessing to an injured, very ill, or very old animal.

"When I decided to have Tess euthanized, it was because she didn't enjoy life anymore, couldn't eat the foods she liked, and couldn't run with the horses. She could barely walk with me up to the mailbox. She hated going to the veterinarian after all she had been through, but we were lucky enough to have one who came to the house—and she didn't have to go that one last time. She was ready to be at peace.

"I wish we humans could be as compassionate to each other as we are to our pets. Because Tess was such an exceptional dog, I know that I will never have another Jack Russell. It would bring back too many memories. I now have a little mix from the pound. His name is O.J. and he is a little master.

"Euthanizing a loving pet is never an easy decision, but at least they can end their lives with dignity."

CHAPTER SIX

BROADENING HORIZONS

Jack Russells like to be busy, and it is in your best interest to make sure your terrier is kept occupied both mentally and physically, to keep him out of trouble. After mastering basic Obedience (Chapter Three), you might like to try something a little more challenging. Here are just a few ideas.

CANINE GOOD CITIZEN

The "Good Citizen" program is an excellent starting point if you want to expand on your Jack Russell's initial puppy training. The American Kennel Club's Canine Good Citizen Program encourages responsible pet ownership and educates dog owners about the benefits of having a well-behaved pet.

Early training and socialization should mean that the exercises for each plan are second nature to your Jack Russell. The key to being successful in the tests is to make sure your dog behaves in a calm, confident manner in a variety of different situations. They include:

- Walking on a loose lead in a controlled manner.
- Walking through a crowd.
- Being approached and petted by a stranger.
- Meeting another dog.
- Being handled and groomed.
- Responding to a number of basic commands.

If a refresher course is needed on the basics, see Chapter Three. There are many participating training clubs in the United States that offer courses to prepare your dog for the tests. To find out more information on the schemes, contact your local kennel club.

AGILITY ABILITY

Agility is an obstacle course to be tackled by your dog within a set time and without faults.

EASY DOES IT

It is dangerous for your dog to exert himself before he is fully grown. The British Kennel Club does not allow dogs to compete until they are at least 18 months old. The American Kennel Club prohibits dogs under one year of age from competing.

The fastest clean round wins. Jack Russells love running around outdoors, getting rid of their excess energy, and most take to the sport very well.

Because of their size, Jack Russells compete in Mini-Agility, where the height of the jumps (including the tire) is reduced, and the long jump is shortened.

Good basic control (see Chapter Three) is essential before you start working with Agility equipment. If your Jack Russell will run with you, and respond instantly to the *recall* regardless of other distractions, it will make things considerably easier when he's first introduced to a course with lots of fascinating scents, and many other dogs running around.

TEACHING COMMANDS

Good communication between you and your Jack Russell is essential for saving time on the course. It is important that your dog is able to interpret your body language, so you must learn always to turn your shoulders to the next piece of equipment that you want your Jack Russell to head to.

Because speed is of the essence, the handler's priority is to run the shortest distance around the course, while controlling the dog through the obstacles. This may mean directing your Jack Russell while you are behind him, in which case he will not be able to see your body language. This is where verbal commands are necessary. To make sure no time is wasted, you always need to be one step ahead, naming the next piece while

Speed is of the essence so commands must be crystal clear.

Photo courtesy: Susan Garrett/ Tein Tran.

your dog is still in the middle of an obstacle. Always remain one step ahead: Vital seconds can be lost by a dog turning the wrong way because the handler didn't direct him in time.

Commands are also needed when "traps" are laid on the course. Traps are obstacles laid in close proximity, putting the owner's handling skills to the test. They are often placed immediately after another element so the dog may assume they form the next part of the course. For example, a tunnel may be placed immediately after a succession of jumps, to make the dog think that is the right route, when in fact he is expected to bypass it altogether. Tunnels are often used as traps, as most dogs—especially Jack Russells—love racing through them. Contact equipment is also popular because treats are used when first teaching it.

There is no standard set of commands for each obstacle. Whatever word you use, make sure it is short, so it can be said quickly and clearly to save time on the course.

Here is a suggested list of commands that are often used.

EQUIPMENT	COMMAND
Hurdles	*"Over"*
Long jump	*"Jump"*
Tire	*"Tire"*
Weave	*"Weave"*
Dog walk	*"Walk"*
A-frame	*"Ramp"*
Seesaw	*"Seesaw"*
Tunnel	*"Tunnel"*

To get your Jack Russell familiar with the commands, use the golden rule of opportunity training and "say as he does." For example, as he is in the middle of leaping a hurdle, command *"Over"* or whatever word you have chosen. Your dog will soon associate the word with the action, and will learn which obstacle to approach according to your verbal command.

The next step is to teach directional commands.

DIRECTION	COMMAND
For the dog to turn to his left	*"Back"*
For the dog to turn to his right	*"Right"*
For the dog to be on your left	*"Heel"*
For the dog to be on your right	*"Rick"*

- The "say as he does" rule also applies when teaching your Jack Russell the commands for turning left or right.
- Send him away and get him to wait.
- Throw a ball to his left or right and tell him to fetch it. As he turns in the right direction to get the ball, give the relevant command (*"Back"* or *"Right"*).
- Practice little and often—on walks and in the yard—as well as at your Agility class, and it will soon become second nature to him.

Traditionally, dogs have always been on the left of the handler, but today there is more flexibility, and dogs run on either side, depending on the quickest way around the course.

Teaching the dog to be on your left or right should be approached the same way as with Obedience heel work (see exercises on page 85). A close heel is not necessary in Agility, but the exercises will get your dog familiar with coming to your side. Once your Jack Russell is running competently on your left side, repeat the exercises with him on your right, repeating the word *"Right."*

OVERCOMING OBSTACLES
Hurdles

This is a very straightforward obstacle, so it is usually the first piece of equipment that is taught.

- Start off with a very low jump. Position your Jack Russell in a *sit-stay* in front of it, and walk around to the other side.
- Call your dog over to you, using verbal encouragement or motivation (treat or squeaky toy). As he jumps, say *"Over"* and give the reward when the jump is completed successfully.
- If your Jack Russell keeps running around the jump instead of over it, put him on a long, loose lead and encourage him over

Despite their small size, Jack Russells have tremendous hurdling ability.
Photo courtesy: Susan Garrett/Tein Tran.

again. After a few successful jumps on the lead, he will realize what he has to do, and the exercise can then be tried off the lead.

- The height of the jump is gradually raised until the dog can reliably clear the maximum required level. In the United States, dogs are assigned a class according to their height at the withers. Most Jack Russells fall into the 12 inches (30.5 cm) category (height of jump) for dogs 14 inches (36 cm) and under at the withers.
- When the jump gets quite high, it is common for dogs to run underneath the pole rather than leap over it. Place a second pole beneath the top one to discourage this.
- Progress to training your dog over a series of jumps.

Long Jump/Broad Jump

In the United States, this obstacle is known as the "broad jump" and is made up of several sections usually placed in ascending order—from the lowest to highest board, making a gradual incline—but it is not an essential requirement. The long jump is 32 inches (81.5 cm) long for Jack Russells and all other dogs who are 16 inches (41 cm) or less at the shoulder. These changes for small dogs have made this fairer for Jack Russells.

- Start with just a couple of sections, removing the rest.
- Get your Jack Russell to sit and stay in front of the jump.
- Stand on the other side of the jump, and encourage your dog over.

Tunnels rarely cause a problem for Jack Russells.

- As he leaps, say your command word *"Long."*
- Reward him with praise, a treat, or a quick play with his favorite toy every time he completes a jump successfully.
- Gradually add sections of the long jump until he can clear all of them.
- Don't forget that as more sections are added, your Jack Russell will need more of a running start to the jump.
- As with the high jump, if your dog runs around the jump instead of over it, a long lead may prove useful.

Rigid (Open) Tunnel

The rigid tunnel is ribbed with hoops, so it remains open all the time. Whereas some breeds can be a little wary of venturing into a dark, unknown area, your only problem as a Jack Russell owner will be getting the little fellow out!

- Scrunch up the tunnel so that it is at its shortest length.
- Sit the dog in front of the tunnel entrance and walk to the other end. You may need an assistant to hold your dog at the tunnel entrance.
- Call your dog through the tunnel, say *"Tunnel,"* and reward him when he runs through. Gradually extend the tunnel's length.
- When he is happy running through the entire tunnel, put a slight bend in it. Bend the tunnel a fraction at a time until it is in the required position.

Collapsible (Closed) Tunnel

This tunnel is made from cloth. The dog has to push his way through it, so it can be slightly difficult to teach.

Most Jack Russells are bursting with confidence, but if yours is a little nervous, take things very slowly.

- Fold the cloth right back on itself, allowing your Jack Russell to see through the tunnel. Encourage him to go through, praising and rewarding when he does so.
- Fold down a small section and call him through. Reward again.
- Once your dog gets accustomed to the feeling of the cloth on him and realizes he has to push through, fold down another section and repeat until he will happily race through the tunnel's entire length.

Tire

As with the jumps, keep the tire low to begin with. You can even begin with it on the ground. As your Jack Russell improves, the height can be raised.

A treat or a toy will encourage your dog to jump through the tire.

- Sit your dog right in front of the tire, and walk around to the other side.
- Hold a treat or toy close to your dog's nose. Slowly pull your hand away from him as he attempts to sniff the treat, and coax him through the tire.
- As he jumps through, say *"Tire,"* or another command you have chosen.
- Give him the treat or the toy as a reward when he goes through the obstacle.
- If he is still reluctant, you can attach a lead, and standing on the other side, encourage him to come through.

Contact Equipment

The "contact" equipment is aptly named, because the dog has to touch a marked section at the start and end of each obstacle. This is to make sure that dogs are not injured by leaping from dangerous heights, and that speed does not forfeit accuracy. A piece of equipment is not considered completed until the marked area is touched.

Dogs are usually initially trained to stop on the marked sections. When they improve and tackle the obstacle at speed, they are then more likely to be preprogrammed to make contact with the area. Because treats are often placed on the contact areas to encourage the dogs to stop, contact equipment soon becomes a fast favorite with most dogs.

Seesaw

Many dogs can feel very unsteady on this piece of equipment, so you must progress slowly, stay close to your dog, and keep reassuring him.

- Put your Jack Russell on the pivot point and praise him when he does not try to jump off.
- When he is happy being on the pivot point, encourage him to take a step forward, down the seesaw. Praise and reassure him the whole time.
- Over the course of several training sessions, extend the distance he will walk down the seesaw. Reward him with every step initially to build up his confidence. Do not let him walk it on his own until he feels absolutely secure on this piece of equipment.
- You can then train your dog to walk up the seesaw, negotiating the pivot point and then down the other side. As he walks it successfully, say your command, *"Seesaw"* so he learns to associate the word with the equipment.

A-Frame

This piece of equipment consists of a steep climb and descent. It has slats to help the dog keep his grip.

- To teach the A-frame, it is easier if it is not "A-shaped" – fold it down so it is just a horizontal board.
- With your Jack Russell at your side, encourage him to run the length of the equipment. Say your command, *"Ramp,"* and reward him when he comes to the end.
- Gradually raise it a fraction at a time, not forgetting to praise him on each occasion, until the frame has quite a marked incline.
- It is important that your dog continues to touch the marked contact points. At full height, the frame is very high, and your dog could injure himself if he leaps to the ground too early.
- As your Jack Russell becomes more confident, and the frame is raised, don't forget that he will need more of a running start to get to the top.

Dog Walk

Although you should teach your dog to walk this piece of equipment, eventually he will race along it, so perhaps it should be renamed the "dog run." It is quite simple to teach, as long as you take it slowly and build up speed very gradually to maintain your dog's confidence.

- With your dog at the start of the equipment and you walking alongside him on the ground, walk him up, across, and down the dog walk, while giving your command, *"Walk."*
- Reward and praise him upon completing the obstacle.
- Keep practicing, gauging his progress and increasing the speed accordingly.
- Be very careful to make sure your Jack Russell touches the contact areas.

Weaving Poles

The weave can be the most difficult piece on the course, and is usually the last obstacle to be taught. Because the weaves are the same width for all breeds, it is likely to take some time for your Jack Russell to go through them at speed. Where the weaves suit a Collie's stride, so that he can just "bounce" rhythmically through them, the Jack Russell has to do a little more running.

There are two ways of teaching your dog.

Method I

- Start with the poles at a 45 degree angle. Alternate the poles, so one is pointing to the left, the next to the right, and so on. Always position the dog so that the first pole is on the dog's left.
- Holding a treat or toy in your hand, lead your dog through the poles and say *"Weave."* Give the treat or toy as you finish.
- Gradually move the poles upright. As your dog weaves through the poles confidently at each level, move the poles

again until he is rhythmically weaving through totally perpendicular poles.

Method II

- Move the first pole to the left and the second pole to the right and so on, until you end up with two parallel rows of poles, about 18 inches (45 cm) apart.
- Encourage your dog to run through them, say *"Weave,"* and reward him at the end.
- Little by little, put the rows closer so they are eventually back in the original one-line weave position and your dog is running through them perfectly.

FLYBALL AND SCENT HURDLING

Both sports originated in the United States, and take place on the same course—a 51-foot

It takes a lot of practice to reach this degree of skill through the weaving poles.
Photo courtesy: Susan Garrett/Tein Tran.

TONTO A PATCH EYE

Hilary Bowden competes in Agility with her three-year-old Jack Russell, Tonto.

"Tonto was nine weeks old when I got him from a shelter, where they had named him Pinto. He had been at the shelter since he was two weeks old, and the staff estimated he had been with his mother for only two days of his life. They said he must have been a very strong puppy to have survived.

"Seven weeks later, I took him home. As all my other dogs, cats, and pony had names beginning with 'T,' I changed Pinto's name to Tonto. When I had to register him with the British Kennel Club (a must to compete in Agility shows), I chose Tonto Λ Patch Eye—I think you can guess why!

"You should start training terriers when they are young, but you should take it very gradually, and shouldn't do anything that is going to cause injury to young bones.

Tonto negotiates the Seesaw, trained by Hilary Bowden.

"The main problem with Jack Russells is that they are easily distracted; they have a limited attention span. Any distraction, and they've gone. I was once training with Tonto and a baseball game was taking place close by, and he just went and joined the game! It obviously looked like more fun than what we were doing. That's the key—to make Agility exciting, so that the dog will ignore distractions and remain focused.

"Tonto responds to treats and squeaky toys. Most Jack Russells do, so it is worth using these as your rewards. We kept training sessions short, and had a game with the ball at the end of each one. We slowly extended the length of sessions, and phased out the rewards—eventually using them only when I knew Tonto's concentration was really flagging.

"The tunnels are a particular area of weakness for Jack Russells—they just love them too much. Show a Jack Russell a dark hole and he's down it! It can be a job in competition to get them away from the tunnel, and it is often used as a 'trap,' where it is put close to another piece of equipment to tempt the dog away from his proper course.

"The answer is to have complete control over your dog, so that he follows your instructions and reads your body signals as to where he should go, and doesn't just do the pieces he enjoys most. Again, this is done by getting him focused and praising him when he does something right.

"The least favorite piece is probably the weaves. Because the gap between them is not shortened for the minis, the weaves do not match their strides. So, whereas a Collie can weave through easily, a short-legged Jack Russell ends up sort of jumping through them and can lose time. The more he practices, the quicker he speeds up and improves.

"Jack Russells are very intelligent dogs and learn quickly. Tonto earned a fifth place at his first show and a first place at his third show. So far this year, Tonto has won 17 rosettes and four trophies.

"When he is not doing Agility, Tonto comes to work with me, so we are rarely apart. I drive a large truck, and he has become known as Tonto the Trucker! Tonto has a great personality—mischievous, happy, cheeky, very bright, but, best of all, very loving."

(15.5 m) long lane. Both Flyball and Scent Hurdling are relay races for two teams of four dogs. In Flyball, the dog must leap four hurdles, trigger a box that releases a tennis ball, catch the ball, and race back over the four jumps to the finishing line—then the next dog runs the course. The winning team is the one that runs the course in the fastest time. If any faults occur (if a dog drops the ball, knocks down a hurdle, or starts running before the previous dog

reaches the line), the dog has to run the course again.

The only difference with Scent Hurdling is that, instead of a Flyball box, there are four dumbbells. Each dumbbell has a colored end (red, blue, green, or yellow), which corresponds to each team member and has the scent of that member, too. After leaping the four hurdles, the dog has to find the dumbbell marked with his owner's scent and bring it back. After each dumbbell is taken, another one is placed on the tray so that each dog has four to choose from.

Jack Russells love Flyball and Scent Hurdling, and are a very popular breed in both sports. Strategically, it is in a team's best interests to have a shorter-legged dog, as the height of the hurdles is fixed according to the smallest team member, and this will make the jumps easier for the other dogs. The jump is placed 4 inches (10 cm) below the smallest dog's height at the shoulder. If that dog is 14 inches (36 cm), for example, the whole team will hurdle 10-inch (25 cm) jumps. The minimum height is 8 inches (20 cm), the maximum is 16 (41 cm). The Jack Russell is often chosen because he is eager, fast, and accurate, and gets results.

Teaching Flyball

The dog has to really want the tennis ball. With a dog like the Jack Russell, it will be impossible to persuade him to take part in a sport unless he cares about the goal—getting the ball. Otherwise, he just will not be bothered. Fortunately, most Jack Russells love tennis balls, so it is isn't too difficult to nurture interest.

A Jack Russell is an asset on a Flyball or Scent-Hurdling team.
Photo courtesy: Teresa York.

SAFETY MEASURES

Only regulation tennis balls in mint condition are used in Flyball. As soon as a ball is punctured or becomes soft, it is replaced.

Never throw a tennis ball in the air for your Jack Russell to catch. If he tilts his head up to grab it and opens his mouth, there is a possibility it could go straight down his throat.

However, there is a danger that overexposure can result in the ball becoming less special, meaning the dog will be less likely to work for it. When your Jack Russell pup is still quite young, you should introduce the tennis ball. Jack Russells are very playful, so it is easy to encourage interest in a game with the ball. It should be made clear that the tennis ball is a special toy. After having a game, it should be put away out of reach. Your pup should have access to other toys, but tennis balls should be out of bounds for everyday play, being brought out only for special games.

According to Flyball organizers, there has been no known case of an accident in the sport involving a tennis ball. Since the ball comes from the side—not from above—it is unlikely to be propelled down the back of the dog's throat. Balls are not released at any great speed, reaching about 2 feet (61 cm) if not caught.

Only when the ball has become a truly desirable object can you start more formal training. It is worth waiting until your pup has grown, as you do not want him to overexert himself while he is still growing.

Teaching Flyball in small, manageable sections suits the Jack Russell's short concentration span. First, the dog is taught to jump over a hurdle, and to come back to the starting line. The hurdles are usually netted, so that the dog has to jump over them; he cannot run around or under.

Blink and you miss it—the Jack Russell shows phenomenal speed when competing in Flyball.
Photo courtesy: Pam Martin.

- Get someone to hold your Jack Russell, while you go around the other side of the jump and encourage him over.
- When he jumps, say *"Over"* and give lots of praise and a treat.
- Keep practicing until he will jump over and back again on voice command alone.
- Progress so that your Jack Russell is jumping two hurdles and then coming back again, then three, then four.

Next, the dog is taught to collect the ball. The box is not introduced until the very end.

- At the end of the four jumps, hold a ball on the floor for your Jack Russell to take before returning over the jumps.
- Hold the ball so that he has to get on the box to take it. This is preparing him for when the box is turned on and he has to trigger the ball.
- Over the course of several practice sessions, gradually move the ball to where it will normally be thrown out by the machine.
- Once he expects the ball to be near the hole, it is an easy transition for him to trigger and catch the ball by himself.
- The machine should be adjusted so the ball comes out slowly, increasing the speed as the dog becomes more proficient.

Noise Sensitive

The majority of dogs that take part in Flyball react to the popping noise of the box. In some cases, the dog's fear can reach a stage where he refuses to go anywhere near the box. Russells are usually quite bomb-proof, but it is better to prevent him from being scared, than to pick up the pieces afterwards.

Most training establishments teach the box only at the very end, when the dog's confidence has been built up and he is happily retrieving the ball from the box area.

You can usually tell immediately if your dog has a problem with the noise. If he is at all apprehensive, the box should be turned off at once. Roll a ball within a few feet of the box and encourage him to fetch it, rewarding him handsomely when he does so. Gradually roll the ball closer to the box until he is confident around it. Never force the dog, or ignore his fear, as it will only make the problem worse.

> **"Do not force your dog or ignore his fear."**

If your Jack Russell becomes afraid of the box, it may be worth taking the box home with you. The last thing you want is for the dog to fear going to Flyball because of the box. If it is at home, too, he will gradually become accustomed to it and should fear it less. Your Flyball training instructor should also have some good ideas about overcoming your Jack Russell's irrational fears.

JACK FLASH

Alison and Wayne O'Rourke have been involved in Flyball for many years, and have branched out into Scent Hurdling. Wayne runs their well-behaved Collies, and Alison runs their wayward Jack Russells, one of which is currently the top Jack Russell in the United Kingdom.

"We have three Jack Russells: eight-year-old Bob, seven-year-old Ted, and six-year-old Spud. The Jack Russell is a fantastic breed, but a lot of hard work!

"We got Ted from a shelter; he had been found on the edge of a roadway—and I can see why! He is wild all the time. He never stops jumping up and down. We have had him five years, and he still hasn't stopped! He can run to the box and back in Flyball in 4.50 seconds, a speed a lot of Collies cannot manage. He is an exceptional dog. At seven years old, he is still very fast and accurate. He does Scent Hurdling in about six seconds.

"Bob was another shelter dog. He was aggressive to other dogs, but he has mellowed—though, he still picks fights in parks. Spud, on the other hand, is a real mommy's boy. He would run all day for me, and really gives his all, but his legs just aren't long enough for him to do really well.

"We also have six Collies and a Lurcher. Jack Russells are not as focused as Collies. They are very easily distracted. If they spot something in the other team's lane, they are likely to run over to it. We get around it by training them while there are a lot of distractions.

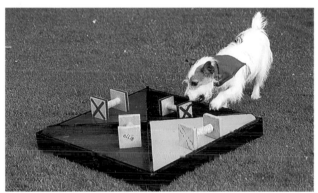

No hesitation—Spud goes for the blue dumb-bell.
Photo courtesy: Alison O'Rourke.

"You have to find something that your Russell really likes, to keep him motivated. Some go mad for a squeaky toy, but the trouble is, whenever someone uses one in the next lane, they are off. We use treats now.

"The other difference between Collies and Jack Russells is that a Collie will do what is asked of him, and do it well. A Jack Russell's outlook on life is that anything will do. Jack Russells tend to pick things up too quickly.

"This isn't a problem in itself, but it does mean they can get bored easily. For instance, a Jack Russell might see a Collie coming to the line with a tennis ball, and instead of racing up to get the ball from the box, he is likely to think: 'Well, why run all the way up there to get a ball, when this Collie has one? It's much easier to get it out of this dog's mouth than to get it out of the box!'

"A Jack Russell is as eager as a Collie, but only on his own terms. When the fun is over for a Jack Russell, the game ends. You can't force a Jack Russell to do anything he doesn't want to do. Years ago, we tried to get one of our Jack Russells to be faster in Flyball. The more we practiced, the slower he got. He was just fed up. You have to train little and often, and stop while he is still fresh.

"Jack Russells love to do something. They are not lapdogs; they are working terriers, and they need something to keep them busy. Flyball and Scent Hurdling helps the likes of Ted and Bob to get rid of their excess energy and anxieties—they run around and bark like mad when about to compete, and it is great at keeping them fit."

TEACHING BOXES

The North American box (which is also used extensively in the United Kingdom) has a pedal making up the whole front face. The dog effectively uses the box as a springboard to turn and continue back down the course, and releases the ball while doing so. The ball comes from the same panel.

The other type used is the British Kennel Club box. It has an arm at the back of the box, which releases a ball once the dog triggers the pedal at the front. This means there are two phases to the dog collecting the ball—trigger and wait. The North American box has a more immediate response to being triggered.

Teaching Scent Hurdling

The hurdles in Scent Hurdling are taught in exactly the same way as in Flyball (see page 80), and the dumbbell retrieval is much easier to teach than the Flyball box.

- Put a board at the end of the jumps, with four color sections (red, green, blue, and yellow).
- A dumbbell with your scent should be placed in one of the sections (if, for a competition, your dog is running last in the team, you might wear green with the dumbbell placed in the green section, so the audience can tell if the dog has successfully collected the right one).
- From his Flyball training, your Jack Russell should be used to fetching an item after the hurdles. If he is reluctant, hold it for him to

take, as you would a tennis ball in the early stages of Flyball training. Gradually lower the dumbbell until he is taking it from the board.

- When he is consistently taking the dumbbell, introduce a second one—without your scent on it (you'll have to get someone else to do this.). Fix it to the tray so that it cannot be taken. This way, your dog can take only the correct dumbbell.
- Keep practicing until your Jack Russell will attempt to take only the dumbbell with your scent. Add another dummy to the board, and then another.
- Once your dog is attempting to take only the correct dumbbell, move it to another part of the board (again, fixing the rest down).
- When your Jack Russell is able to identify the correct dumbbell consistently, wherever it is placed on the board, then you can detach the others.

COMPETITIVE OBEDIENCE

Jack Russells are nowhere near as commonplace in the Obedience ring as Collies, German Shepherd Dogs, or some of the gundog breeds, but they do have something to offer. Jack Russells are a lot smarter than most people give them credit for; the problem is that they become bored with the Obedience ring because everything is so uniform and the sequence never changes. You need to show your Jack Russell that Obedience is a fun game. The moment you become too serious is the moment your Jack Russell will lose interest.

Being working dogs, these industrious little terriers like to be kept occupied, and Obedience certainly does that.

Heel

Jack Russells were bred to work with people, though often independently from them. The Jack Russell thinks for himself. It is not a natural trait in him to cling slavishly to his master. For this reason, heelwork is more difficult to teach than with, for example, a Border Collie. The Jack Russell is also so much shorter, which makes it more difficult to keep track of his movements, and to build up that all-important handler/dog bond and closeness.

The main problem with teaching heelwork is to get your excited Jack Russell to walk beside you with all four feet on the ground. He is more likely to jump up at you for some attention, or to race ahead after an interesting smell.

Before starting, practice the exercise on page 45. Having worked on getting your puppy to walk beside you in a well-mannered way, you just need to do some fine-tuning.

- Stand with your dog on your left side. Hold some food in your left hand, with your arm next to your leg, so the dog can smell it.
- Your Jack Russell's head should be at your knee. When he is standing in the correct position, say your command word—such as *"Close"* or *"Watch"*—and give him a treat.
- Start off by taking a few steps and reward your Jack Russell for taking just one step in the proper position. Guide him with your hand; because he knows it contains a treat, he will probably be watching it like a hawk. If he goes too far forward, guide him back into the right position, say *"Close,"* and start again.
- Keep practicing, gradually increasing the number of steps. Remember that short sessions are better than long, repetitive, boring ones that are not going to keep your dog's interest. At the end of each session, have a fun ball game.

The Jack Russell is more than capable of competing in Obedience.
Photo courtesy: Linda Barden.

Retrieve

Pam Martin has been training and teaching dogs for more than 20 years, and owns an Obedience training school in the Dallas area. When teaching Obedience, she uses a new training technique called Backward Train Chaining, a fast and easy method of dog training that not only suits most people's busy lifestyles, but is also ideal for the Jack Russell personality. As she says, "Our eager-to-learn Jack Russell Terriers will agree that fast and fun is the only way to train."

Backward Chaining uses food and positive reinforcements, and teaches a chain of behaviors in the reverse order to which it will be performed. "Teaching a *retrieve* backwards is by far one of the fastest and also easiest methods you can use on puppies, with little to no stress on them," says Pam. "Most *retrieve* methods teach the *take it* first, but not so with this method. To teach the *backward retrieve,* we start with the *out,* which is the last command in the chain of commands for a *retrieve. Take it* will be the last command taught, which is the first order your dog will hear in the chain of events for a *retrieve.*"

It sounds confusing, but, in practice, it is very simple. Here are Pam's tips for training a five-month pup. The steps work equally well on adult dogs.

Out

- The puppy needs to be hungry so he will be receptive to the soft, yummy treats you will be using for rewarding the right behaviors.
- You will also need to use something soft for the puppy to put in his mouth, such as a soft ball that fits in his mouth easily.

Your puppy may be teething, and harder objects may cause pain. Train only on days when you see your puppy is using his mouth without reluctance.

- Get down on the floor with your pup and have treats ready in a shirt pocket. The food is out of sight but your pup will know that treats are near, as Jack Russells have a keen sense of smell.
- Gently put the ball in the pup's mouth and allow him to immediately expel it while you say *"Out,"* and give him big praise and a food reward. If you place an object into an untrained dog's mouth, chances are high that they will reject it fast. This is not a problem and is quite normal behavior; just praise and reward.
- Repeat several times, placing the ball in the mouth and waiting for it to be expelled into your hand. Repeat the command *"Out"* as the act of releasing is performed.

Hold It

The next step in the chain is for the pup to *hold it* until he hears the command *"Out."*

- As you place the ball in his mouth, gently hold his muzzle closed, just enough so the ball won't come out.
- Hold closed for an instant and then command *"Out,"* quickly praise, and reward.
- Again hold the muzzle closed just a second longer, slowly increase the time from one second to two seconds, then three seconds and so on.

The retrieve should be taught as a series of exercises.
Photo courtesy: Linda Barden.

- You can praise him while he is holding the ball, but make a big fuss over the *out* command, praising him highly.

Touch It

Touch it is not a command—you will never say these words, but it will become a new behavior the pup will learn to offer separately from the *out* and the *hold* commands.

- Start this session by holding the ball high in the air as if you are admiring an object of great value.
- Slowly lower your hand, showing the ball to the pup, and praise and reward him for simply looking at it.
- If the pup makes any contact with the ball, that is great—exactly what you want, so praise and reward!
- Get him excited about seeing the ball in your hand, but do not give any commands yet.

Allow him to touch the ball with his nose if he likes. If he doesn't try to make contact, accidentally bump him—very gently—with the ball and make a big fuss over the ball touching his nose.

- After a few sessions like this, the pup will soon be touching the ball with his nose or pawing at the ball. All the while, praise him for his efforts.
- When you are sure that the pup understands that making contact with the ball is the right behavior, and, in doing so, expects a food reward, then you know you're on the right track.
- Lower the ball to the ground. Keep your hand on it and wait for the pup to make contact with it. Praise and reward him. Be sure to make this exercise fun.

Take It

Once he is doing this behavior consistently, you have to get the puppy to pick up the ball from off the ground.

- Only use the *take it* command when you're sure that it, the *take* behavior, will happen—if the pup goes to snap it up every time you put the ball on the floor.
- Tell the pup to *"Take"* just as he performs the behavior on cue, and add back the remaining commands in the chain of events, the *hold* and then lastly the *out*.

Proofing

Once you have taught the behaviors, you need to "proof them"—make the commands stronger

TEX SUCCESS

Starkweather Dusky Jem—or Tex—has more letters after his name than the average brain surgeon: CGC, TT, AAD, NA, EAC, EJC, OGC, RS-O, JS-O, GS-N. The five-year-old holds multiple Agility titles and has two qualifying scores toward both his AKC (American Kennel Club) and ASCA (Australian Shepherd Club of America) CD (Companion Dog) titles. But, as owner Linda Barden explains, success didn't come overnight.

"Tex came home with me on April 6, 1994, and his training began five days later. At the age of eight weeks, Tex was on his way to learning the basic facts about Obedience. *"Sit"* and *"Down"* came easily for this little 5-pound (2.3 kg) package, but we had a lot of work to do on the *come* command.

"We began our training through a six-week puppy kindergarten class at a local dog training facility. Tex was the smallest dog, but many people would comment on how quick he was to

The quick-witted Jack Russell can compete on equal terms with the more conventional Obedience competitors.   **Photo courtesy: Linda Barden.**

learn. I have to say, Jack Russells are one of the smartest breeds I have ever worked with, and, as an Agility instructor, I have worked with a lot of different breeds.

"After successfully graduating puppy kindergarten, Tex and I went on to a Level 2 Obedience course, where we were instructed and taught the skills needed to pass a Canine Good Citizen test. During the CGC test, the dog and handler are put through a series of tasks that simulate situations the dog may run into in everyday life: *"Sit"* and *"Down"* on command, *"Stay,"* *"Come"* when called, walking on a loose lead, and many other similar tasks. At five months of age, and at about 7 pounds (3.2 kg), Tex was walking away from his second Obedience class with his first title, CGC.

"Since then, Tex and I have participated in a number of different Obedience classes where we work on tasks we have already learned and improve them to a competitive level. It wasn't an easy or a quick process by any means.

"I think Tex was two-and-a-half before I even did an Obedience fun day. We had a difficult time getting through the off-leash heeling exercise—he is a Jack Russell and loves to use his nose, slowly wandering away from me to find the source of that wonderful scent.

"In 1998, when the Jack Russell was recognized by the AKC and put into the Miscellaneous class, Tex and I began competing in both AKC and ASCA competitions toward our Obedience titles. Our first two ASCA legs came quickly; a lot of time, patience, and practice had finally paid off and I thought, 'Wow, this is going to be easier than I thought.' Then Tex remembered he was a Jack Russell.

"We have had a number of times where we have failed to pass during competition.

Whether it is that tempting squeaky toy outside the ring, or the spayed female sitting nice and quietly next to him, Tex would seem to find some way to really humble my ego. Some trials would start off with wonderful individual workouts, just to have Tex get tired of lying next to that yellow Lab and want to play during the final task of the three-minute *down*. So close, but yet so far away. Humiliating? Sometimes. Fun? Always—I wouldn't change it for the world!

"Our first AKC qualifying score was accomplished in January 1999. Not only did Tex and I qualify with a score of 192 (a qualifying score is 170 or above out of 200), but Tex would be the one to take home the first-place blue ribbon. So much for the Labs, Collies, and Shepherds in the ring with us— here was a Jack Russell Terrier taking home the blue.

"In total terrier spirit, Tex gladly grabbed hold of his leash and played tug throughout the whole awards ceremony. We received our second qualifying score in July 1999 with a 'humbling' 172 out of 200. This was an exciting day because Tex and I shared the ring with another Jack Russell: Kimberly Baker and her dog Riley qualified and took fourth place with a qualifying score of 182.

"It's a rare occasion that you see a Jack Russell in the Obedience ring, but it's worth the attention from everyone when you can go out there and show everyone how it can be done. The Jack Russell is a wonderful dog, and, with a lot of time and patience, I think a Jack Russell could do just about anything. Anyone who owns a Jack Russell will tell you how wonderfully intelligent the breed is. If you want them to know how to do something, show it to them once—they'll figure it out from then on."

Scenting the correct article is an extension of the retrieve.   *Photo courtesy: Susan Garrett.*

by showing the dog under what conditions he must perform them: where and for how long he must hold the ball and what happens if he drops the ball. This is the trial and error stage where your Jack Russell learns the important concepts for each chain of events. He learns that he gets nothing if he fails to perform the last part of the behavior, placing the ball in my hand—the *out*—and, in order to do that, he must pick up the ball from the ground.

Before long, you can place the ball on the ground and move away from it, just a step or two in the beginning, until you are some distance away. The pup now has to *go* and *take* and, as he returns, you command *"Sit,"* for him to sit in front facing you.

Finally, throw the ball out and the pup will have only one thing on his mind—the final part, the *out,* which ends in praise and rewards.

It is your job to keep the training simple and fun. Learning can be stressful, so remember to always be patient and to have fun with your Jack Russell.

FREESTYLE

Canine Freestyle, or Heelwork to Music, is an offshoot of Obedience, where the dog and handler adapt traditional Obedience moves to "dance" or to move gracefully to music. It is fun to do and to watch, and is becoming increasingly popular, both in the United States and the United Kingdom.

Because it is not yet recognized by the British KC and the AKC, there are no universal rules for this new sport; they vary according to the Freestyle body organizing each show. Generally, a dog and handler move around the ring in the *heel* position, incorporating jumps, spins, leg-weaves and numerous other types of moves in the routine. The ring is usually about 40 feet (12 m) by 80 feet (24 m).

The owner can choose any piece of music as long as it falls within the time frame given—usually anywhere between two and six minutes in the United States, and three and four minutes in the United Kingdom. The team is scored according to its technical execution (precision, degree, or accuracy, etc.) and artistic flair (choreography, costume, etc.).

Transatlantic Differences

There are slight variations between the rules in the United Kingdom and the United States. Freestyle is known as Heelwork to Music in the

DANCES WITH DOGS

Kay Richards, a breeder and exhibitor, has considerable experience in training Jack Russells. She has trained two Russells for the hearing-impaired, and has also tutored her dogs in Obedience, Muskrat Racing (racing in water), and Agility. Now she has turned to Freestyle.

"When I first saw Freestyle, I was totally in awe," says Richards. "I did not realize that Freestyle was an art form; I thought it was just another form of training. I can remember sitting there watching the dogs and handlers, and thinking: 'God, this is beautiful. I wonder if my dog and I could do that?' So we joined a class.

"I start my pups in conformation around four to six months of age," says Richards. "This gets them used to going out in public, to walking on a loose lead, and to paying attention to me. I also take them to training or socialization classes so they become familiar with playing with other breeds of dog. Jack Russells tend to think that anything that isn't a Jack Russell must be prey! Then, before they are a year old, I put them in an Obedience class.

"Ebony was my first Freestyle dog and the required moves came slowly at first because I did not know what I was doing, but now I show her what I want, and, as soon as I get the desired response, I will click the behavior, treat her, and put a word to the behavior, such as *"Stay."* Then I will ask for the behavior again, click, treat, and name the behavior. I will then immediately go to something else, usually something she is really good at to boost her confidence and to end the training on a positive note.

"The next day, when I ask for that new behavior, she will give it to me faster, and I will make a big fuss over how well she's done it. If she doesn't do it right, I will move back to a behavior she can do well, and will quit while I'm ahead. Jack Russells are sensitive and intelligent creatures, and if I have learned anything in dog training, it is to make sure that training stays fun.

"The music is picked for the rhythm of the dog. For Ebony, I have to make sure it is light enough for her. She is small, so flutes, pianos, and guitars are good for her stride. A large breed of dog can look good walking to trombones, but not Jack Russells. Instrumentals seem to work better, as words tend to detract from the performance.

"Costumes can be a distraction, too. The Canine Freestyle Federation (one of several Freestyle bodies) wants to see the dog move and perform Obedience to music, and does not really care for costumes. However, we do try to wear clothing that complements the dog's colors, and try to send a message to the audience. I try to look a little like a court jester, as it fits my music—*Pie in the Face Polka* by Mancini, which sounds almost like circus music.

Kay Richards uses clicker training for Canine Freestyle. Photo courtesy: Kay Richards.

"I think Ebony enjoys Freestyle because it is our time together. However, owners have to work to overcome the Jack Russell extreme prey drive. This is a real distraction for them, both in training, and as a pet. The only solution is work, work, work. First of all, I concentrate on their ground sniffing. Attention training is good for this.

"At least five times a week, I will take Ebony and just walk around with her on my left and right side. Whenever she looks up at me, I will feed her. She has to look right at me before I give her a treat. When we first started, I would click her and treat. Now I just say 'Yes' and treat. The word 'Yes' is as strong as the click, but it takes longer to use the word 'Yes' than to click. However, it is useful in performing and class situations in the absence of the clicker.

"The attention problem we are now having is that Ebony has become extremely sensitive to noise. This is inherent in my lines (I have been breeding for 12 years). I started with a line that was very easy to train and submissive toward people. They make wonderful pets, but shut down if spoken to harshly or if they encounter a loud noise.

"Now, each week, I spend time in the class just doing rhythm heeling, with my classmates making all sorts of noises. Each time I see my dog flinch, I feed her something very special (cheese, sausage, etc.). Eventually, she should start to associate the loud distraction with something good, and forget about it. Plus, the attention training is going to have to continue for some time.

"Freestyle is a team sport. The dog feeds off your energy. If you are down and tired, the dog will perform that way. Trust in both of the partners has to be 100 percent."

United Kingdom. As with Obedience, more emphasis is placed on precision and accuracy.

THE WORKING TERRIER

Love it or hate it, there is no denying the Jack Russell's working past. Times and opinions about hunting may have changed in the last several hundred years, but the Jack Russell's instinct to work has not. As an owner, this is something that you will have to live with. Even if you never intend to work your terrier, you will have quite a job stopping him from going off after a rat or a rabbit, or charging down a hole.

Although it is becoming less popular, and is threatened with legislative change in the United Kingdom, hunting is enjoyed by many terrier enthusiasts who work their dogs on hunts, a job the Jack Russell was originally bred for. The role of the Jack Russell is to go below ground in search of a fox, or other legal quarry. He can bolt the fox so a hunt can continue, or so that the animal can be killed (as by shooting). Alternatively, he can bark to alert the terrierman of the quarry's location so that it can be dug out and killed. The Jack Russell should not engage with the fox; doing so could cause injury to both animals.

Other legal quarry in the United Kingdom includes mink, rats, and rabbits. Legal quarry in the United States varies from state to state. Generally, groundhog and possum are legal in most states, but, being fur-bearing animals, the red fox, gray fox, and the raccoon are protected in some states. Your working terrier club will have information on what is legal in your state.

A TERRIERMAN TALKS

Brian Male is chairman of the Jack Russell Terrier Club of Great Britain, and has worked Russells for most of his life.

"I have been interested in working terriers for about 40 years," says Male. "As a child, I had a young Wire-haired Fox Terrier. I was with my father on a farm one day and a hare jumped up. The terrier chased it around in circles and eventually caught it. We had it for our dinner later that week, and I have been hooked ever since.

"Since then, I have worked on all types of quarry, and was an amateur terrierman for six years. I continue to do fox control for farmers and gamekeepers. I have a small farm, and my Jack Russells are an effective means of pest control—either they chase rats away unharmed, or they kill them quickly, a knack that forms part of their basic instinct.

"A terrier is such an unusual character, and has so many excellent qualities that others don't have. He is happy on a windy hillside in the rain, or on someone's lap in front of the TV. The Jack Russell is everything someone wants out of a dog, and adjusts to every situation.

"Working them lets them do what they were originally bred for. Whether you take them hunting, or let them chase an old sock in the backyard, they will love every minute of it.

"A good working terrier must have stamina and intelligence, and should have a good coat to withstand any adverse weather conditions above

Brian Male with his team of working Jack Russells.

the ground, as well as harsh terrain below it. He should have a strong jaw to defend himself against attack, and the flexibility to move freely—to turn around in the hole, and to back off from the quarry if necessary. Above all, a working Jack Russell should have an excellent temperament, and should be able to be handled by anyone at any time. He shouldn't be aggressive at all—to people or to other dogs.

"I work 12 terriers and each one has his own personality and strengths; you get to know which dog to use in each situation. Some are better below ground, some above; some won't stay with the quarry, giving it the opportunity to bolt, which is fine if you don't want to dig it out. Each situation is different.

"The age at which you start preparing a Jack Russell varies—some grow faster; some may be slow learners. Experience tells you when they are ready. There is no formal training as such: They watch and learn from the other dogs, and gradually, their instincts come out. They have to enjoy what they are doing—you can't make a dog do something.

"I work primarily to enjoy my dogs. I love my terriers—they are great friends to me, no matter what. Working them enables me to see so much of the countryside and its wildlife, and I have made some of the greatest friends through the dogs. On top of this, I have all I have ever wished for—the love of my dogs."

If you are interested in working your Jack Russell, you must join a recognized working terrier club, which will give you help and advice.

SHOWING YOUR JACK RUSSELL

Every owner thinks his or her dog is a winner, but it takes more than good looks to win a judge's heart in the show ring. Conformation shows aren't just beauty shows; they are there to improve the breed by showing the best examples and encouraging others to attain the same standards.

If you want to show your dog seriously (not just at fun shows), you have to make sure your Jack Russell is registered with your national Kennel Club, or has parents that are. In the United Kingdom, the only type of Jack Russell officially recognized is the Parson Russell Terrier.

Although you might improve as a handler, there is little you can do to make sure your pup grows into the ideal specimen of the breed. Nature must take its course. An experienced

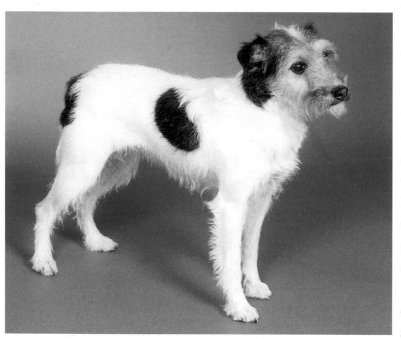

Every owner thinks his or her dog is a winner—but you need to be confident your Jack Russell conforms closely to the Breed Standard.

breeder develops an eye for what has show potential, so you should tell them exactly what you want out of a puppy before buying. Remember, though, that breeders are not fortune-tellers, and can never guarantee that a pup will be a winner in the future.

With an older dog, you should also consult a breed expert (contact your Kennel Club for local club details) to be sure you won't be wasting your time showing a substandard Jack Russell.

You should also be prepared for the time and effort involved in showing. Fortunately, with the Jack Russell, preparation for a show is minimal (no fussy coat care, as with some breeds), but showing is a serious commitment, and involves a great deal of traveling. Entry fees, travel, and accommodation costs all add up, so be prepared for the expenses involved, too.

However, the show circuit soon becomes a way of life for many exhibitors—their hobby as well as their social life. Seen in this light, the expense is more than justified. It is somewhere you can meet like-minded people, make good friends, and share your pride in your dog. If you win, that's a bonus. If you don't, at least you've still had an enjoyable day out.

Show Ring Training

Once your pup has had his puppy vaccinations, you should enroll at a ring training class. It is excellent preparation for both handlers and dogs. As well as teaching you how to stand and walk your pup to his best advantage, the class is a great socializing experience for your Jack Russell; he will learn to interact with other dogs, to accept being examined by the judge, as well as being taught what is expected of him in the ring.

Take your pup for just short periods at first, and build up as he gets older and his confidence grows.

Standing

At ring training, you will be taught how to stack your dog. He should be stood foursquare, with his head and tail up. If they won't stay up naturally, put your hand under them to hold them up.

When your dog is in the right position, say *"Stand,"* wait for a few seconds, and then praise and reward. Gradually build up the time he is expected to stand. With time, he will learn what position is required when you say *"Stand,"* and this will make things much easier in the ring.

Examining

Once the judge has assessed the overall appearance of your dog, he or she will compare your Jack Russell against the Breed Standard (see Chapter Eight), examining your dog's body to make sure he has the right skeletal conformation, coat, teeth, balance, etc. Your dog should be relaxed while this examination takes place. Remember that your dog is also being judged on his temperament, and it will not be in his favor if he snaps or growls at the judge. Early socialization with many different people should get him used to being handled (see Chapter Three).

Moving

The judge will also want to see your Jack Russell in action, and will indicate where he would like you to walk with your dog. The Jack Russell should move straight, in a

With luck, your puppy will mature into a typical specimen of the breed, and will learn the skills of showmanship.

SHOW GIRL

Tracey Stark got bitten by the showing bug from exhibiting her parents' Bulldog. When her husband, Martin, suggested getting a Jack Russell, Tracey was insistent that it should be one that was recognized by the British Kennel Club, so she could take up showing again. They have been showing Sally, a Parson Russell Terrier, for three years.

"Sally was a real horror at her first show. She was just so pleased to be there that she went berserk," says Tracey. "She was just hanging on the lead, and the judge couldn't get near her. We went to different training classes to get her used to other dogs, and found one that was terrier-oriented, and she's fine now. It just takes time to settle them down.

"Outside the ring, she loves everyone and wants to make friends, but inside the ring, she knows exactly what to do, and behaves perfectly well. She's now got two fourths at Championship shows under her belt.

"I have a seven-week-old puppy now, that I am also hoping to show as soon as she is 13 weeks old. I'll take her to ring training classes to teach her how to stand, and to get her used to other dogs. It's also a good idea to get the dog used to being handled by as many people as possible, so they will accept a judge examining them. Ring training is also for the owners—to teach them what to do—as well as the dog.

"Because the Parson hasn't been registered for very long in the United Kingdom, it is exciting to be involved in a breed from the start. Although it is quite new to the world of showing, numerically the breed is very strong, and competition is very stiff.

"When you first start showing, you should be thick-skinned. You might be top of the line one day and bottom the next, so you have to learn to take the rough with the smooth. You also get better at showing your dog to the best advantage. Martin shows Sally quite a lot, and he's really improved from when he first started.

"Showing is addictive. Once you get into it, it's like a drug. It's not just the winning; it's being part of it. You make some very good friends, and get to see them at the different shows. Some people say: 'But don't you get bored doing the same thing every week?' But it's not the same: You see different people and your dog might perform differently each time. It's just good fun."

It was Sally who gave Tracey Stark the showing bug.

Terriers love the thrill of the chase.
Photo courtesy: Brian Male.

well-coordinated way, and with his head up. Many handlers use a short show lead, to encourage the dog's head to stay up, but others—with more amenable dogs—use a looser lead.

TERRIER RACING

Terrier racing is a great way for Jack Russells to channel their high energy without leaving a trail of carnage in their wake. For this reason it is enjoyed not only by hunting enthusiasts eager to encourage their dogs' chase instinct, but also by those who are fervently opposed to hunting, yet still respect their Jack Russell's working heritage.

Terrier racing involves six dogs racing each other on a straight track of between 150 and 300 feet (46–91 m), in pursuit of a lure. A number of 8- to 16-inch (20–41 cm) hurdles may be placed on the track, the height will be dependent on the age and height of the dogs

competing. The top dogs can run a 300-foot (91 m) track in 10 to 15 seconds. In the United States, most terrier races are exclusively for Russells; in the United Kingdom, Russells can compete against a number of other diverse terrier breeds, depending on the organization putting on the show.

For details of your nearest racing club, contact your breed club.

Puppy Practice

It is easy to tell quite early whether a Jack Russell will be a good terrier racer. The physical attributes are not as important as the dog's temperament. Although longer-legged dogs usually make faster racers, temperament is the key feature. An outgoing, willing dog that enjoys playing and chasing can be developed, but a shy or timid Jack Russell rarely becomes successful on the track—or enjoys it.

THRILL OF THE CHASE

David Miller enjoys watching racing as much as his dogs enjoy doing it. His first racer, Odie (named after the dopey dog in the Garfield cartoon), was an exceptional racer, becoming a National Champion at just 11 months old. Since then, Miller has been hooked on the sport.

"When racing, the dogs enjoy themselves and have a good time, and I enjoy the uncertainty of what can happen in a race. You could have a Champion racing that looks likely to win, but a trip at a hurdle or a collision with the other dogs could produce an entirely different outcome.

"When Odie became a National Champion, it was a very proud moment for me. He was competing against a dog that had beaten him in two races in previous weeks, so we didn't expect him to win.

"He was a great racer. At 15 inches (38 cm), and weighing 21 pounds (9.5 kg), he was a big dog—and was very focused. We race the dogs with muzzles so that if there is a dog that isn't as focused in the race—and that tries to start a fight—none of the dogs can come to any harm. If any dog tried to pick a fight with Odie, you should have seen his expression! He'd pull his ears back and look at the dog as if to say: 'Look, we're here to have fun—and anyway, can you see how big I am?' He was such a big, powerful dog.

"As soon as Odie got in the box, he would start flailing about. We wear shirts especially for racing, as they get scratched to pieces when we put the dogs in the box, and, for the Nationals in 1993, we had bruises on our chests from where Odie was so excited.

"We used to hunt with him occasionally, but racing is much safer for the dogs. The first time he got his first groundhog, he ended up with a gaping wound in his paw. Groundhogs can kill a terrier—they have real claws and large front teeth—and foxes can do some damage too.

"Sadly, Odie was killed last year, at the age of six. He had escaped over the garden fence and was hit by a car. Many hunting and racing dogs end up being killed this way.

"We are now racing Moose, a son of Odie, who is doing well. Odie has about seven children and grandchildren that are racing, so he's certainly left his legacy."

CANINE FRISBEE

The sport of Canine Frisbee has been around in the United States for roughly 25 years now. Initially, the dogs were judged on the height and style of the catch. Today, it's still judged on catching, but more disks are added for the dog to catch and the handler is involved more, adding as much flair as possible.

Lou Mack (pictured) is a professional Frisbee competitor, who has twice won the world title. Jack Russell "Air" Max is an adoption dog that Lou acquired from a kennel in California. He is now one of the best performing dogs in the disk dog world.

Lou Mack has taught Max a number of spectacular tricks, including Max doing a handstand in the palm of Lou's hand (below), and where he backflips over another dog or person while catching a Frisbee (below right). Photos courtesy: Lou Mack.

CHAPTER SEVEN

A SPECIAL BOND

The Jack Russell has lost none of his working roots. An industrious little worker, he loves—and needs—to be kept busy, both mentally and physically. Although his size precludes him from some areas of assistance work, such as becoming a Guide Dog for the Blind, he is an ideal candidate in other areas of canine service.

Assistance dog organizations have found that, although the Jack Russell is not suitable for placements where physical strength is a necessity, the Jack Russell's diminutive size is actually an asset in the right circumstances. Candidates for assistance dogs come from all walks of life. Some may not have the space for a large dog, so a Jack Russell would suit them better than a German Shepherd Dog or a Golden Retriever.

Smaller breeds also make day-to-day living simpler—for example, they can fit into the smallest of cars.

The costs of keeping a Jack Russell are less too. He will not eat as much as a larger breed (though some Russells will try to persuade you that this is not the case!), and veterinary care will also prove less costly.

HEARING DOGS

Shape and size are of no significance when it comes to recruiting hearing dogs that work as assistance dogs for the deaf. Their job is to alert their owners to everyday sounds. The Jack Russell has many desirable qualities, as Claire Guest points out.

"Jack Russell Terriers have a quick, alert nature that makes them ideal dogs for response to sound. Fast on their feet, they work tirelessly and never fail to respond day or night—they always keep one ear open. Hearing Dog work is only suited to those individuals that do not display a strong hunting drive, and those that have a sociable nature with both humans and other animals."

SCAMPI'S NEW LIFE

Jean Lawrence will certainly testify to the Jack Russell's friendly nature. Her Hearing Dog, Scampi, is a tricolored Jack Russell type that has improved her life immeasurably.

"In common with many Hearing Dog recruits, Scampi came from a shelter, so his early background is unknown," says Lawrence, who has about 95 percent hearing loss. "However, he showed the alertness to sounds, the enthusiasm for being with people, and the gentleness necessary for being a Hearing Dog that could accompany his recipient in all sorts of situations.

"After his period of socialization, he was trained to alert me to the alarm clock, cooker timer, doorbell, door knock, telephone and fax, smoke alarm, intruder alarm and carbon monoxide alarm. He was also taught to *'Call Jean,'* for when my family wanted me, or to *'Call Gerald,'* to help me call my husband.

Jean Lawrence's life has been transformed by Scampi. Photo: Studio Norwich Photographers.

"After Scampi's training, it was my turn to learn to care for him and to respond appropriately when he alerted me to 'our' sounds. This is where I discovered that inside my little dog, there is a big dog waiting to leap out! He is so enthusiastic about his work, that sometimes he needs to be gently reminded that, when I am sitting or standing, he should touch me on the knee and not on the shoulder as he must do when I am lying down!

"Once home, we became very close, as we practiced the sound work and Obedience training, and enjoyed the walks and grooming—and the cuddles! We were proud when we passed the assessment (which tested whether we were working properly), and Scampi received his yellow jacket showing that he is a Hearing Dog.

"Scampi is my ears. He provides me with information about 'our' sounds, which is important, as it has given me independence again. It has also enabled me to contribute to family life in the same way that I used to. Scampi's Jack Russell playfulness and pride have helped to increase my confidence, and have given me the freedom to live life as fully as when I could hear.

"Scampi is also my best friend and accepts me as I am; we communicate easily with each other. He can lift me out of my emotional doldrums, as I cannot resist his look or his nudge and gentle lick. His body language shows that he can enjoy my laugh, but he realizes that using his voice has no effect on me.

"I think Scampi is fantastic, but I admit to being prejudiced because he has changed my life so positively. Is he perfect? Well, to me he is— and his own style of doing things helps to keep us alert.

"He used to chase rabbits (not unusual for Jack Russells, I believe!) but I rewarded him each time he saw, but did not chase, one. In time, he learned to come to sit in front of me to watch them.

"Occasionally, his overzealous nature persuades him to be overanxious in alerting me to a sound. Once he led me through a supermarket to the doorbell display where someone was trying out 'our' doorbell! Plus, he is a real jumping Jack. Some mornings he leaps from his bed onto mine without even touching the floor to alert me to my alarm ringing. In addition to the touch on the shoulder, he gives a lick on my cheek, as he is wide awake and very pleased with himself.

"The very gentle side of Scampi's nature shines through when he senses that I am not well, and also when he accompanies me to schools and youth groups, where I talk about his work. He loves being with children.

"Scampi is very special to me. I had felt very close to my pet dogs, but nothing could have prepared me for the strength of love that I have for Scampi. In return, he benefits from the constant companionship that we share.

"He enjoys coming with me to places that are closed to other dogs (shops, for example) and laps up the attention he receives. His expressive face says 'Call me irresistible'— but those of us who know him really appreciate that his Jack Russell nature is reflected in his name, Scampi."

THERAPY DOGS

Therapy dogs visit hospitals, hospices, and residential homes, spending time with the sick or elderly. Studies have shown the therapeutic value that animals have on people, and a visit from a pet can bring happiness and pleasure to people who are living in institutions, isolated from the outside world. Volunteers who visit people with their pets perform an invaluable service to a wide range of people of all ages.

Jack Russells are very inquisitive and generally enjoy new experiences and meeting new people, so it is no surprise that they make popular therapy dogs. Being small, they can easily get on someone's lap or bed, and are easy to cuddle with. Their outgoing personalities, coupled with their friendly natures, make them an overall hit.

A RAY OF SUNSHINE

Anne Graham has taken Peggy, her six-year-old registered therapy dog, on visits to a children's hospital ward, and a residential home for the elderly for nearly three years.

"I heard about the work of therapy dogs from a friend who had read an article in the press. As a dog lover, I thought it sounded like a good idea. Patients in the hospital often miss their pets, and many people in residential homes are not able to take their pets with them, so a visit from my dogs could be popular, I thought.

"Peggy has all the right qualities for a therapy dog: She is very good-natured, loves people, and has the perfect temperament for the job. I also have a Labrador Retriever that is a registered therapy dog, but Peggy can actually get on a patient's bed or lap.

"Jack Russells are great fun and are very addictive. Labs are stoically good-natured, steady, and dependable, and the fun thing about Jack Russells is that they are not! They are full of life. Fortunately, Peggy is always calm and gentle on her visits, and takes her duties very seriously. Like all therapy dogs, she had to pass a temperament test before being registered, and be fully inoculated and wormed.

Peggy visiting the children's ward.
Photo: North of England Newspapers.

"When we walk through the hospital to the children's ward, you can see everyone's faces when they see the dogs. It isn't just the patients—nurses and visitors all have silly grins on their faces when they see us trotting up the corridors.

"Peggy's visit breaks up the long day for the patients or residents. She is a real morale booster. She will help a patient forget his or her illness or discomfort, calm his or her fears, and sometimes helps to dry a few tears. A visit from Peggy helps to brighten a long day.

"Thankfully, few children in the hospital stay for long, so we may not see the same 'customers' more than once. However, we do see the same elderly residents every week, and are able to build relationships with them. They stroke Peggy and tickle her tummy, while talking about the dogs they once owned.

"Peggy loves her work, and feels very important trotting along on her lead. It is an added bonus if there is a tidbit here and there during the visit.

"I know how lucky I am to have the fun of Peggy in my life, and I am pleased to have the opportunity to share her with others."

DOGS FOR THE PHYSICALLY CHALLENGED

Larger breeds, such as the Labrador or the Golden Retriever, dominate the world of assistance dog work with the physically challenged. Their size and strength enable them to perform more tasks than the Jack Russell.

However, that didn't stop Chris Cox from training her own Jack when she was diagnosed with multiple sclerosis. An experienced Obedience trainer from Minnesota, Cox has trained Daisy to assist in all areas of her life.

DAISY DOES IT ALL

"I was diagnosed with multiple sclerosis four and a half years ago and was pretty bad for a while," says Chris Cox. "While visiting some horse friends (I breed, train, show, and sell reining horses), my husband, Dale, and I met their new Jack Russell puppy. On the way home we got to talking about getting a dog that could keep me company while Dale was working and I was housebound, but that could also keep up when I was working outside all day with the horses.

"My Daisy has been all that and more! She seems to know when I am not feeling well and will not leave my side. Daisy is the first dog I have ever trained, and the first I have ever considered showing. We went through two organized Obedience classes, but mostly we have trained at home during our 'normal' days. Our Obedience instructor has had us demonstrating at schools and community events, and prompted us to start to show when the Jack Russell Terrier was UKC-recognized. (The UKC, United Kennel Club, is the second largest all-breed dog registry in the United States.)

"We were the only Jack Russell at the shows, and she earned her UKC CD (Companion Dog) with three first places. She got her UKC CDX (Companion Dog Excellent) with two firsts and one second before she was 20 months old. Daisy was also the first Jack Russell Terrier to earn an American Kennel Club Obedience title.

"I suppose I have to credit Daisy's assistance and therapy help at least partly to her Obedience training, but it has all seemed to come so easily to her. Daisy has helped me from the beginning by just being there. She is such a comfort and will just sit all day when that's all I can do (not typical for a Jack Russell, I know now!). When I get depressed, she will go to all ends to make me laugh with her silly antics and excessive kisses.

"Daisy will 'find Dad' (my husband) and bring him back to where I am, whether we are at home or in public at a horse show. She will bring me my slippers, sweatshirt, remote control, phone, or anything she can lift that I can point to if she doesn't 'know' it. When I drop something (I am always throwing horse brushes around because I lose my grip on them while brushing), she usually gets the brush automatically and brings it back to me.

"With all the help she has given me, I wanted to share her with others, so when the local Therapy Dogs International group held a test, we attended with both Daisy and my male, Whip. I know now that the other dogs there had all attended classes for this, but neither Whip nor Daisy had any trouble passing the exam, probably because the examiners couldn't throw anything at them that I hadn't already!"

"Daisy and I are on a list for a pilot program for Pets Enabling People, in which people with disabilities train their own assistance dogs, but as I do not drive and my husband works a rotating shift, it is difficult for me to get to classes (over an hour's drive). The other dogs/handlers are not anywhere as advanced as Daisy and I in Obedience, so they are trying to work something out so we can join in when the group has 'caught up' to us.

"If this program works out, and if I eventually do become more independent, Daisy could actually become a licensed assistance dog with the lawful right to accompany me any-where (like a Seeing Eye dog). As she is just four years old, and is from a long-lived family, this is one thing that keeps me sane when things get really bad.

"Daisy just loves to visit schools, nursing homes and hospitals. She seems to know when people do not want so many kisses (Daisy loves to kiss) and calms down with the more fragile patients and just lets them pet and talk to her. Whip is best with just a cuddle. He loves to cuddle and will push his head softly but persistently into the person's hand until they start to pet him. He also loves to play ball with the kids, but really it's the cuddle that he craves.

"Daisy also does some 'tricks' to entertain, and loves to show off.

Daisy is a tremendous help and comfort to her owner, Chris Cox.
Photo courtesy: Chris Cox.

"One of her favorites is 'spinning' like a reining horse. All of our reining patterns call for four spins; Daisy 'counts' and will spin four times.

"Daisy is well known at our horse shows as she loves to ride horses. Whenever I am on a horse or my husband is, she just cannot wait until we get off, so she can ride. Daisy is always the first one to get on my young horses. The babies get used to her sitting on their backs before they are weaned. (She actually *asks* to get on these guys, really!)

"I have three Jack Russells now (Hannah has joined us), and they all live with me 24 hours a day and sleep in our bedroom at night. They are 'my children' and are all spoiled, but they also all have their Obedience titles.

"I cannot imagine what life would be like without my dogs. They are always there to keep me company and truly help me with everything I do through the day. Some days it is hard just to get out of bed in the morning, but when that persistent little nose tells me she *has* to go outside, I get up, and things don't seem as bad as they could be. They are always willing to play or cuddle, and so willing to do whatever I ask of them. Plus we no longer have a woodchuck or gopher problem on our farm since we got the Jack Russells!"

CHAPTER EIGHT

SEEKING PERFECTION

Every Jack Russell is unique, his own individual personality crafted from a combination of genes and upbringing. At their core, however, most Jack Russells share certain breed traits—whether it is their physical conformation or their unmistakable terrier personality. This "Jack Russellness" forms the basis of the Breed Standard, a written blueprint that defines the ideal Jack Russell that every breeder strives to achieve.

BETTER BREEDING

People have bred dogs for particular jobs for thousands of years—whether that is for hunting, guarding, herding, droving, or as companion dogs. By breeding dogs with desirable traits (whether physical or temperamental), many different types developed, from the diminutive Chihuahua to the imposing Great Dane.

However, over the years, the dog's primary role has become that of companion. Some dogs still work, of course, but the majority are kept simply as pets. With so many breeds so far from the tasks for which they were originally bred, Breed Standards are vital to make sure each breed remains true to type. Without a precise

The aim of every breeder is to produce puppies that conform as closely as possible to the Breed Standard.

description of the ideal specimen of each breed, there is a danger that breeders could lose sight of the reasons why a certain breed has particular qualities. If these qualities or characteristics are not appreciated, they will not feature in the breeding program—and they can easily be lost forever.

THE BREED STANDARD

The Breed Standard is not only used by breeders to be sure dogs remain true to type; it is also the standard against which a breed is judged in the show ring. Consistent winners in the ring are sought after to produce or sire future generations in order to keep the traits in the breed.

The Breed Standard below is a composite summary of the AKC Jack Russell Terrier Standard and the KC Parson Russell Terrier Standard, and looks at how the Standards relate to the Russell's working heritage. The Jack Russell Club of Great Britain, although not recognized by the KC, has its own particular Standard, which is slightly different. The dogs are very similar in appearance, but the main difference is over the issue of size—dogs from 10 to 15 inches (25–38 cm) are permitted. For a copy of the official Standard applicable to your country, contact your national Kennel Club.

General Appearance/Characteristics

Both the AKC and the KC stress how the breed is a working terrier that should have the ability and conformation to pursue his quarry underground and run with hounds.

The Jack Russell should have a workmanlike appearance, built for speed and endurance.

Scars from "honorable" work are permissible, to ensure that the feisty working nature of the breed is not penalized in the ring. If scars were not allowed, it could result in the show and working split that so annoyed the Parson John Russell. Injuries and scars from such work or accidents are permitted by the AKC "unless they interfere with movement or utility for work or breeding."

Temperament

The Russell should be bold and friendly. Additionally, the AKC describes his two "personalities." While working he should be "a game hunter, tenacious and courageous," and at home with his family he should be "playful exuberant, and overwhelmingly affectionate." He should not be quarrelsome.

Head And Skull

Flat and fairly broad, becoming narrower to the eyes. The nose must be black.

Eyes

The almond-shaped eyes should be dark and display a keen, alert expression. To avoid injury when working, they should be fairly deep-set, and not protruding.

Ears

The small V-shaped ears (of moderate thickness) drop forward and are carried close to the head.

Mouth

Teeth should meet in a complete scissor bite, meaning the top teeth closely overlap the bottom teeth. This, together with strong jaws, ensures the Russell will be able to pull quarry from the ground if necessary.

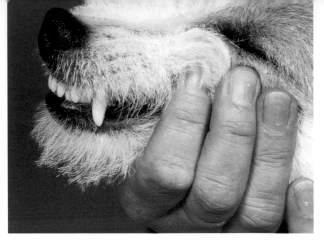

The jaws are powerful, and the teeth meet in a complete scissor bite.

Neck

The muscular neck should be a fair length and gradually widen to the shoulders. The dog was meant to bay at the fox, but if he did get into trouble with a fox down a hole, he needed a long enough neck to protect himself with his teeth.

Forequarters

Shoulders should be long and sloping (a terrier with upright shoulders walks with a stilted movement). The elbows should be close to the body, working free of the sides to enable the dog to stride out.

Body

The KC suggests the dog's overall length is slightly longer than the height from the withers to the ground. The AKC states the dog should be 1 or 1.5 inches taller than he is long.

The chest should be of moderate depth, and should be able to be spanned behind the shoulders by hands of average size. There should be plenty of room for the heart, but a dog with a deep rigid chest would be unable to get to ground, or could get stuck if he did get in.

The expression is keen and alert.

The elbows are close to the body to allow the dog to stride out.

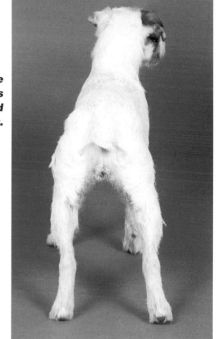

The hindquarters are strong and muscular.

The back should be straight and strong, and the loin slightly arched. A short-backed dog would not be able to turn around in small places—a vital requirement for an "earth dog."

Hindquarters

Powerful hindquarters are needed to drive the dog forward when in pursuit of quarry. They should be strong and muscular "with good angulation and bend of stifle" (AKC and KC).

Feet

The compact feet should have tough pads to protect them. They should face forward, turning neither in nor out.

Tail

The tail should be strong and set fairly high. It is customarily docked and should provide a good handhold, with which, traditionally, the dog was pulled from ground.

Gait/Movement

The Russell should move freely, and in a well-coordinated manner, with a straight action in front and behind. Any other action is uneconomical and would slow down the dog's movement.

Coat

The coat should protect the dog from the elements and from any hazards, such as briar, when out working. It should be waterproof, dense and harsh—whether smooth-coated or broken/rough-coated. Because of its protective function, it is important that the coat also covers the belly and undersides of the thighs —the areas that are particularly exposed to undergrowth when the dog is working.

Color

The KC states the dog should be white or predominantly white with tan, lemon or black markings. The AKC allows "white, white

The coat must protect the dog from the elements, whether it is smooth-coated (as above) or broken/rough-coated.

This broken-coated Jack Russell has ideal markings—on the face and at the root of the tail.

with black or tan markings, or a combination of these, tricolor," and also allows grizzle.

In both the KC and the AKC, it is preferable if these markings appear on the head and/or root of the tail.

Size

The ideal height for a dog is 14 inches (35 cm), and 13 inches (32.5 cm) for bitches. An inch (2.5 cm) above or below the ideal height is acceptable provided the dog looks well balanced and conforms to other areas of the Standard.

PUPPY TO CHAMPION

It is never easy to predict which pup will make it as a show dog. The basics of the Breed Standard can be applied to a pup at eight weeks, but that is only the beginning. It could grow too big, too tall, too long, or it could lose its scissor bite when the adult teeth grow through.

An experienced breeder usually develops an eye for what qualities to look for when assessing a litter, but pups can always surprise you. One that shows great potential at eight weeks may not develop as well as expected, and by six months, it may be clear the dog does not have a destiny in the show ring or as breeding stock. Equally, a pup that showed no promise, and was sold to a pet home, could turn into a showstopper.

The following photos show the development of a Jack Russell pup through the different stages to becoming a Champion and upholding the Breed Standard.

PUPPY TO CHAMPION

Photos courtesy: Marcia Walsh.

▲ Snow Winds Hailey pictured at nine weeks.

▲ Four months.

◄ Seven months.

Snow Winds Hailey—now an ► American Champion.

CHAPTER NINE

HEALTH CARE

Trevor Turner BVetMed, MRCVS

Jack Russells are basically working terriers and, like many working dogs, are relatively free from inherent problems. This chapter outlines some of their more common conditions, details important areas of preventive care, and has a brief section on first-aid in the event of an emergency.

PREVENTIVE CARE

Although small in size, Jack Russells are not sedentary by nature and therefore require a reasonable amount of exercise on a daily basis. Otherwise, no matter how conscientious you are with diet, obesity can result. In the short-legged, hunt-type Jack Russell Terrier, this can lead to joint problems and ultimately, arthritis, as well as other problems of the joints.

Regular exercise has to be considered part of preventive care. A walk during a midsummer evening is one thing, but battling through icy November rain in gale-force winds is quite another. To our four-legged friend, it is all part of life's rich pattern, and he will be just as eager for the winter walk as the summer one. Sorry, it really is just as necessary!

Despite all the best efforts with diet control, some dogs, like some people, inevitably grow fat with age. These dogs still require regular exercise, but it has to be adjusted to the individual. In this case, it is better to reduce the distance and possibly increase the frequency of outings. Also, avoid the heat of the day in summer. You would be surprised at the number of dogs seen trailing behind their owners, obviously laboring under the stress of the midday sun, something that would never have affected the very same dog when younger. Remember that dogs age just as we do. Unfortunately, they do it quicker.

Vaccination

Vaccination (inoculation) stimulates the dog to produce active immunity against one, or a collection of diseases, without developing any signs of disease. A puppy initially acquires some immunity from the dam (mother) via the bloodstream, while in the womb, and then after birth, from the mother's milk, while nursing. This is called *acquired immunity*. Once weaned, this immunity fades, and vaccination should take place.

Primary vaccination usually starts at between six and ten weeks of age, and may involve several injections approximately two to four weeks apart. The timing of vaccination and the vaccine used will vary depending on disease prevalence in the area, and other risk factors. Once you have acquired your puppy, it is worthwhile calling local veterinary clinics and asking them about their vaccination policy. At the same time, you can discuss appointment details, prices, and facilities, and whether the practice organizes puppy classes. These are socialization classes, and they can be very helpful in the case of Jack Russells, as interaction with other dogs may be problematical as the dog matures. Puppy socialization classes will often avert trouble and should be regarded as part of preventive care, particularly for the novice owner.

The Question of Boosters

Vaccination is unlikely to last indefinitely, and regular boosters are therefore advised. The question is: How often?

Originally, it was considered the safest policy to boost against all diseases every year. Recent concern regarding the possibility of some dogs developing reactions to booster vaccination has led to a new way of thinking.

Vaccination courses usually start between eight and ten weeks.

It is possible that some of the boosters are unnecessary. My personal view is that the risk of reaction is so slight, compared with the threat of the disease in the unprotected dog, that I would go for annual boosters every time.

This is based on clinical experience. While in practice, I encountered distemper, hepatitis, and then, in the 1980s, parvovirus, in epidemic proportions. Despite working and living with dogs all my life, I have never had to treat a dog with a serious vaccine reaction.

I readily concede I may be biased, but having run a busy veterinary hospital for many years and not seen a severe vaccine reaction, I can only ask: How common are they in reality? If in doubt, discuss the matter carefully with your veterinarian. The time of the primary vaccination course is a good opportunity. Whatever you do, make sure the first protective vaccination course is administered, since it is then that the puppy, once maternal immunity has waned, is at the greatest risk.

Blood tests are available that will reveal the immune status of the dog for any of the diseases against which we regularly vaccinate, and indicate if revaccination (boosting) is really warranted.

Adopting a blood-testing procedure can be expensive, since the blood test for each disease will probably be as much as a combined booster against all the diseases.

Consider also the stress caused to the dog by adopting such a procedure. Taking a blood sample for most dogs is considerably more stressful than a booster vaccination, which is a simple subcutaneous (under the skin) injection.

Some vaccines by their very nature do not have a long-lasting immunity. For example, intranasal *Bordetella bronchiseptica* vaccines against infectious tracheitis, or so-called kennel cough, last approximately eight months. If you are regularly boarding your dog or going to training classes, biannual revaccination (boosting) against this condition is well worth considering.

Leptospira vaccines are usually routinely included in the primary vaccination series. These are killed bacterial vaccines and provide a workable immunity in the average dog for only about 12 months.

> **❝ Core vaccines give protection against fatal diseases. ❞**

Modified live virus vaccines, such as distemper or hepatitis, give a much longer period of protection, but this varies with the individual. Due to the efficacy of the so-called multivalent (multidisease) vaccines and the scarcity of concrete evidence in respect to the adverse effects of boosting, little work has been done to establish exactly how necessary or how often revaccination should be carried out.

If you have anxieties regarding booster vaccinations, take time to discuss the matter with your veterinarian.

Because of the concerns expressed regarding vaccination and the number of components in multivalent vaccines, there is a move in the United States to divide vaccinations into two groups: core vaccines and non-core vaccines.

Core vaccines are necessary to protect against a disease that is serious, fatal, or difficult to treat. In the United Kingdom, these include distemper, parvovirus, and hepatitis (adenovirus disease). In the United States, rabies is also a core vaccine (and possibly in the United Kingdom in the near future).

Non-core vaccines in the United States include *bordetella*, *leptospirosis*, *coronavirus*, and *borrelia* (Lyme disease), since this latter vaccine is known to cause reactions.

Contagious Diseases

● **Canine distemper** is no longer widespread solely due to vaccination. It presents with a variety of signs (symptoms). Fever, diarrhea, coughing, discharges from the nose and eyes are

If you have any concerns over booster vaccinations, discuss them with your veterinarian.

all seen. Sometimes the foot pads harden—this is the so-called "hardpad" variant. A high proportion of infected dogs develop nervous signs—fits, chorea (twitching of muscle groups) and paralysis.

- **Canine hepatitis** (adenovirus disease) has been successfully combated via vaccination. Signs can vary from sudden death with acute infection to mild cases where the patient is just a bit off color. In severe cases, there is usually a fever, enlargement of all the lymph nodes (glands), and a swollen liver. During recovery the dog can develop "blue eye" and may look blind due to edema (swelling) of the cornea (the clear part in the front of the eye). Although initially cause for worry, this usually heals without lasting effects.

- **Canine parvovirus** (CPV) is caused by a virus that can exist in the environment for a long time. It reached epidemic proportions in Europe and North America in the 1980s. The main signs include vomiting and diarrhea, often with blood (dysentery). Undoubtedly, control of the disease has been due to the development of highly effective vaccines.

- **Rabies** vaccination is mandatory in many countries, including the United States. With the relaxation of quarantine in the United Kingdom, which is at present rabies-free, rabies vaccination may well become mandatory. Recently, the vaccine has become readily available to veterinary clinics. The disease is communicable to humans (zoonotic), and although prevention by vaccination is extremely successful, the same unfortunately cannot be said for treatment, either with dogs or people.

- **Bordetellosis**, or infectious tracheitis, is not usually life-threatening except in very young and old dogs. It causes a persistent cough. In the United Kingdom the bacterial organism *bordetella bronchiseptica* is the usual primary cause, although viruses can also be implicated. In the United States, the parainfluenza virus is usually the main cause, with bordetella a secondary invader.

Multivalent vaccines, both in the United Kingdom and in the United States, today often include a parainfluenza component. The bordetella component is usually administered separately through nasal drops, which have been shown to give better

*The dog flea—
Ctenocephalides
canis.*

External Parasites

Fleas

These are probably the most common external parasite found on dogs, and the Jack Russell Terrier, with his love of the great outdoors, is no exception. Some dogs will carry very high flea infestations without showing any signs, whereas others can develop a flea allergy dermatitis from being bitten only once. Fleas are not host-specific; therefore, both dog and cat fleas can be found on dogs, cats, and humans. Wild animal fleas can be a problem on dogs in suburban gardens where wild animals are common. Human fleas are very rare, but all types can bite humans as well as other animals.

Effective flea control involves both adult fleas on the dog and also the immature stages that develop in the home. Fleas have to have a meal of blood to complete their lifecycle, so they feed on the dog, but eggs develop in the environment. Development of the next generation depends upon temperature and humidity, and can be as short as three weeks. Fleas can survive in suitable environments for more than a year without feeding. This is the

but also parasite control, both for **ectoparasites** (lice, fleas and ticks), and **endoparasites** (worms—tapeworm, roundworm, and some of the other less common species, such as hookworms).

Jack Russells are, at heart, country dogs. Thus, fleas, lice, and other ectoparasites can cause problems, depending on where you live and your pet's lifestyle. Therefore, a scratching Jack Russell should perhaps be investigated at the outset a little more carefully than some other breeds.

Initial itching, which may have a simple cause, such as fleas or a grass allergy, can sometimes result in skin conditions in the Jack Russell that can prove difficult and expensive to clear up.

Since these dogs are hunters and are not averse to eating their prey, worms and other endoparasites can also be a problem unless a prevention plan is conscientiously applied.

reason why dogs—and people—can be bitten when entering properties left unoccupied for some time.

Control in the home should include thorough vacuuming to remove flea eggs and fleas. You should also use an insecticide with a prolonged action to kill any developing fleas, since few insecticides currently on the market kill flea larvae.

Treatment of your dog can be in the form of oral medication, which prevents completion of the lifecycle of the flea, as well as applications in the form of sprays or powders, which kill any adult fleas present. Insecticidal baths are effective at killing adult fleas in the coat, but do not have any lasting effect.

Bathing should be combined with other methods of flea control. Spot-on treatments are very popular, too. They use very sophisticated technology to disperse the chemical without getting in the bloodstream. The chemical is in a vehicle that spreads through the fat layer on the skin very quickly: Within 24 hours, the dog will have total protection against fleas for approximately two months. When a flea bites the dog, it penetrates through the fat layer to get to the blood, and then ingests the chemical. The dog can be bathed several times without the efficacy of the treatment being affected.

Lice

Lice can be a problem but are not as ubiquitous as fleas and usually require direct contact for transmission. Unlike fleas, the whole lifecycle

Dogs living in the country pick up ticks from sheep.

occurs on the host, and the eggs (nits) are attached to individual hairs. Infestation is usually associated with violent itching. Bathing in an ectoparasitical shampoo is an effective treatment.

Ticks

Ticks can be troublesome in some areas. In suburbia they are frequently carried on wild animals, whereas in rural areas, livestock can be the primary host. In America, ticks are the carriers for Lyme disease. As with fleas and lice, there are a variety of insecticidal products available, some of which have prolonged activity even if the dog is bathed in between.

Walking Dandruff

This can sometimes be a problem in Jack Russell Terrier puppies, particularly if they have been bred on a farm or some other rural location.

Walking dandruff, (or *Cheyletiellosis*) is an apt description. The pup will be itchy, particularly along the back and sometimes the underparts, with a lot of dandruff visible. This "scurf" sometimes appears to move. The actual small scalelike white mite is just visible with the naked eye. Treatment with any of the extermal parasite preparations results in a rapid cure.

Harvest Mites

These are tiny, red, larval mites that occur in late summer and fall and can affect dogs exercised in fields and woodland locations. They cause intense irritation and can be seen with the naked eye as tiny red dots. The head as well as the dog's feet can be affected. Insecticidal sprays or washes result in rapid eradication.

Internal Parasites

The most important endoparasites, as far as your Jack Russell is concerned, are worms. There are other protozoan parasites, such as *Coccidia* and *Giardia,* but these are not as widespread.

Roundworms

Roundworms are virtually parasitical, particularly in puppies. The most common roundworm is *Toxocara canis*. It is a large, round white worm 3–6 inches (7–15 cm) long.

The lifecycle is complex, and puppies can be born with a *Toxocara* worm burden acquired from their mother before birth. Roundworm larvae remain dormant in the tissue of adult dogs. In the bitch, however, under the influence of hormones during pregnancy, they become activated, cross the placenta, and enter the puppy, where they finally develop into adult worms in the small intestine. Larvae are also passed from bitch to puppy during nursing.

Today there are many effective worm treatments. Veterinarians advise regular worming of litters from approximately two weeks of age, and treatment is repeated regularly until the puppy is at least six months old.

Because there is a slight risk that humans can become infected with roundworms from dogs, adult dogs should be wormed about twice a year. Effective preparations are on sale in supermarkets and pet stores, but it is always worth discussing a worming strategy with your veterinarian.

Although some adult dogs can carry heavy worm burdens if not regularly wormed,

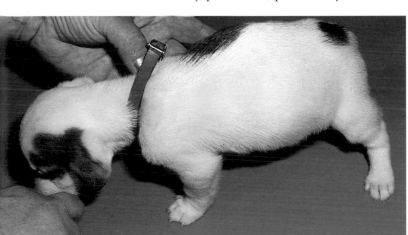

A Jack Russell puppy showing the typical potbelly that indicates a roundworm burden.

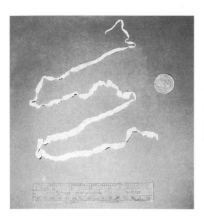

Tapeworm passed by an adult dog. (The coin gives an indication of size).

surprisingly few show symptoms. In the puppy, however, a heavy infestation with roundworms can cause many problems, from generalized ill health to diarrhea, vomiting, obstruction of the bowel, and even death.

Tapeworms

The other major class of worms are cestodes, or tapeworms. Unlike roundworms, they do not have a direct lifecycle, so spread is not directly from dog to dog. Intermediate hosts vary from fleas to sheep, horses, rodents, and sometimes humans, depending on the type of worm.

The most common tapeworm in the dog is *Dipylidium caninum*. Fleas are the intermediate hosts. Flea larvae swallow tapeworm eggs shed by the dog in the feces. These mature as the flea develops. The dog consumes the flea and so the lifecycle is completed. *Dipylidum* is a large worm and can measure up to 20 inches (50 cms). Individual tapeworm segments, which are passed in the feces, resemble small rice grains around the dog's anus. Effective tapeworm treatments are available, but it is important that fleas are also controlled.

Other species of tapeworm have intermediate hosts that can include sheep, horses, rodents, and even humans. The species will infect your dog only if raw meat of the infested intermediate host is fed, or if the dog manages to ingest dead animal carcasses.

Tapeworms are usually found in the adult dog and although it is aesthetically unpleasant to see tapeworm segments wriggling out of the anus, tapeworm infestation, unless very heavy, has surprisingly few effects on the mature, healthy dog.

Other types of worms affecting the bowel include hookworm (*Ancylostoma*) and whipworm (*Trichuris*). These can be a problem, particularly in kennel dogs that have grass runs, but modern multiwormers usually contain components to combat these species.

The canine lungworm (*Filaroides osleri*) most commonly affects puppies and young dogs. The worm lives in nodules in the air passages and can cause coughing and loss of condition. Remedies are available from your veterinarian.

Heartworm is caused by a roundworm (*Dirofilaria immitis*). It is a large worm of up to 11.5 inches (30 cm) in length; its larval form is transmitted by mosquitoes.

Today there are very effective remedies to prevent the onset of heart failure, which at one time was only too commonly seen in infected dogs.

EMERGENCY CARE AND FIRST AID

Jack Russell Terriers are inquisitive, active extroverts and sometimes accidents occur. These include injuries from being hit by a car, bites and fight wounds, burns and scalds, heatstroke, poisoning, and insect stings causing severe allergic reactions. Emergencies can also arise as a result of seizures or acute shock. Jack Russells are great investigators, and it is not uncommon for them to fall down holes,

All dog owners should learn basic first aid.

shafts, cliffs, etc. Sometimes, acute hemorrhagic gastroenteritis strikes a normally healthy dog and he will suddenly develop watery, bloody diarrhea.

Regardless of the emergency, there is much that can be done via simple first aid. In an emergency, you should do the following:

1. Keep calm and do not panic.
2. If possible, get help. Contact your veterinarian, explain the situation, and get first aid advice.
3. If there is a possible injury, keep your dog as still as possible. With a Jack Russell, this is easier than with the larger breeds.
4. If in shock, it is important to keep the dog warm. Try wrapping him in a blanket, and cradling him in your arms.
5. If there is a possibility of fractures, particularly of the spine, lay the dog in a box and cover him with a blanket. Try to keep him as quiet as possible.
6. Take your dog to the veterinarian as soon as possible. Drive carefully and observe the speed limits!

First Aid

First aid is the initial treatment given in an emergency immediately after injury, collapse, or sudden onset of illness.

The purposes are to preserve life, reduce pain and discomfort, and to minimize the risk of permanent disability or disfigurement by preventing further damage.

First aid is essential if your Jack Russell experiences: fits and/or unconsciousness (collapse); breathing problems; bleeding and/or shock.

Shock is a complex condition and is difficult to define. It always results in a serious fall of blood pressure.

Causes include:
- Loss of blood volume due to bleeding
- Heart failure
- Acute allergic reactions
- Heatstroke

First signs of shock include:
- Rapid breathing
- Rapid heart rate

The Jack Russell is a hardy dog, and suffers very few hereditary problems.

- Paleness of the mucous membranes of the gums, lips, and under the eyelids
- Vomiting
- Severe depresssion
- Cold to the touch, particularly the feet or ears

Shock is involved in many first aid situations. Warmth is important. Keep the animal quiet and seek immediate veterinary help, particularly if there is any bleeding, which you should endeavor to control.

Airway

If your Jack Russell has vomited and collapsed, or is choking, make sure the airway is clear. Do not put your bare fingers in the mouth. Remember that the dog will be just as frightened as you are if he is fighting for his life, and may bite with panic.

It is sometimes possible to open the mouth using a blunt instrument and to remove any foreign material.

If your Jack Russell is not breathing, try gently pumping the chest with your hand, at the same time feeling just behind the elbow to see if

you can feel a heartb
massage can be tried.
the sternum, gently s
heart, just behind the
pulled slightly forward

If the emergency is
accident, handle your
him in a box or basket,
veterinarian as soon as
warm by wrapping him

Bleeding

If bleeding is severe and
bandage can be applied
material. A polythene ba
limb will keep the blood
wound can then be bandaged over.

On certain parts of the body, such as the head
or neck, a tight bandage may not be practical.
Instead, covering the bleeding area with a clean
pad of material and applying finger or hand
pressure will help to stem hemorrhaging until
assistance is available.

Burns and Scalds

Cool the burned area with cold water as quickly
as possible. Cover with damp towels. If the
burn is due to a caustic substance, wash as much
of it away as you can with plenty of cold water.

Heatstroke

In warm, humid weather, heatstroke can rapidly
occur. It is a frequent result of dogs being left
in cars with too little ventilation in hot weather
over 65°F (18°C). Remember that the car need

solution). Get to the veterinarian promptly.

Fits and Seizures

Your Jack Russell is not likely to swallow his
tongue if he has a fit, so do not interfere with
his mouth. The less he is stimulated by the
owner, the better. Ideally, place him in a dark
confined area where he cannot damage himself.
This will speed recovery. A cardboard packing
case is ideal for a dog the size of a Jack Russell.

Most fits last only a few seconds or minutes,
and it is better to wait until the dog has recovered
a little before going to the veterinarian. If a fit
continues for more than three or four minutes,
contact your veterinarian immediately.

BREED-SPECIFIC CONDITIONS

Active, energetic dogs, Jack Russells suffer few
of the hereditary problems that affect many

...metimes these glands become impacted and infected, and form abscesses. This is an extremely painful condition for the dog and is not uncommon in the Jack Russell. The usual signs are excessive attention being paid to the back end or dragging the anus along the ground (scooting). If you notice these signs, consult your veterinarian without delay.

some of the conditions to which Jack Russells are especially prone.

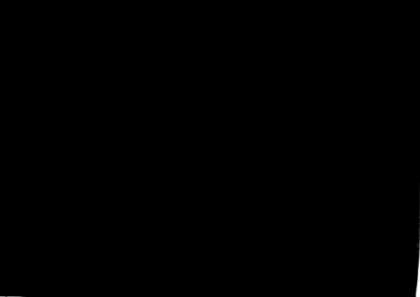

The short-legged Jack Russell sometimes suffers joint problems.

Allergic Skin Diseases

Fleas have already been discussed. Many Jack Russells develop a hypersensitivity reaction to fleas and other causes. They can develop allergies due to causes, such as grass pollen. If your Jack Russell appears excessively itchy, particularly in spring and summer, consult your veterinarian before spending too much money on flea preparations!

Anal Glands

On either side of the anus, there are two small scent glands. They occur in both male and female dogs. This is one of the reasons why dogs sniff each other's backsides when greeting each other.

Bone Disorders

Parson John Russell developed his terriers to hunt fox and to keep up with his hounds, and it was from this sound, healthy stock that today's Jack Russell Terrier has evolved. The short-legged, broad-chested, smooth-coated Jack Russell can sometimes suffer some joint problems, such as slipping kneecaps, (medially luxating patellae). Although they respond well to special surgery, individuals with these joint problems should not be bred, despite the fact that, in many cases, these conditions may be acquired because of their lifestyle rather than due to inherited factors. With some longer limbs, Jack Russells are particularly sound little dogs and rarely suffer these problems.

Digestive Upsets

Jack Russells love to hunt. Decomposing animal carcasses—rats, mice, and rabbits particularly—have a special attraction, so it is not surprising that vomiting occurs. If a digestive upset is transient, and the dog is otherwise alert, do not allow him to drink too much at any one time, but offer small quantities of fluid (ideally water) frequently. You may need to take no further action except perhaps not feeding him for 12 to 24 hours.

If diarrhea develops and the pet is still alert, feed a light diet, such as chicken, fish, rice, etc., for 24 to 48 hours.

If vomiting and/or diarrhea persists, or if there is any sign of blood, contact your veterinarian immediately. (See Emergency Treatment and First Aid).

Docking

Jack Russell Terriers are not born with short tails. Traditionally, the tail was shortened to prevent injury when entering rabbit burrows, etc. At the same time it was not cut off completely, as the handler, when hunting with the dog, used the short tail to pull the dog from any holes where it had become stuck. In many countries today, docking is banned—but tradition persists, and show dogs in the United Kingdom and the United States are customarily shown with docked tails.

Problems can arise from the shortening of the tail. The most common problem is that the tail is a little too short and, when the dog sits down, he can hit the end of it on the ground. This can cause inflammation and infection, which is difficult to heal and sensitive to the touch. If your dog appears to be showing a lot of interest in the end of the tail, and it appears red, sore, or swollen, consult your veterinarian.

Another common problem with the docked tail is that during healing, the small piece of bone protrudes from the skin and irritates the dog. Sometimes this may require minor surgery.

Excessive Drinking (Polydipsia)

Certain signs in your dog can be due to more than one cause. If your Jack Russell suddenly starts to drink a lot, this can be due simply to thirst as a result of exercise or hot weather. It can also be a sign of problems such as incipient kidney disease, bowel upset, possibly diarrhea or vomiting, or a serious disease such as diabetes.

Eye Problems

Primary glaucoma is a disease in which pressure inside the eye rises, and it can cause rapid blindness. This is due to an inherited defect, whereas **secondary glaucoma** may be due to other causes, such as injury. Primary glaucoma is not uncommon in Jack Russell

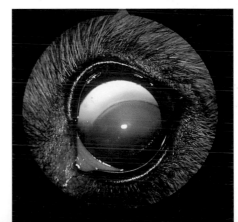

Anterior lens luxation.

Terriers, and the eye can become blind because of the increased pressure on the optic nerve.

Lens luxation can also occur in the Jack Russell. The lens, suspended inside the eyeball, serves to focus images on the light-sensitive surface, the retina, at the back of the eye. Without a lens, it is impossible to see clearly. In the Jack Russell it is not uncommon for the lens to dislocate from its normal position behind the iris. This is due to an inherent weakness in the ligaments fixing the lens. Usually the lens will move forward through the iris and will then block the drainage of fluid from inside the eye. **Secondary glaucoma**, i.e., increases in pressure within the eyeball, then develops.

These conditions require urgent veterinary attention. Specialist veterinary ophthalmologists can operate to reduce the intraocular pressure or to remove the dislocated lens and avoid total blindness.

Obesity

Obesity is a problem in any of the small pet breeds, particularly as they grow old, and the Jack Russell is no exception. As exercise tolerance decreases, and treats become more plentiful (most people spoil their older pets), the resulting increase in weight puts more strain on joints, heart, and lungs, and the dog tends to exercise even less.

Do not think that if your dog is overweight, exercise must be increased. Talk to your veterinarian about what he or she would recommend. In some cases, overexercise can be seriously detrimental to your pet's health.

Orthopedic Conditions

Jack Russells can sometimes sustain joint injuries, particularly to the knee (stifle joint). If your dog does become lame or appears to have a sore, swollen joint, consult your veterinarian. Many orthopedic operations performed by specialists can prevent permanent disability.

Prostatic Disease

Male Jack Russells, particularly as they age, can develop an enlarged prostate gland. The first signs of this are usually difficulties with urination or defecation. The condition responds well to early treatment.

Neutering (see Chapter Four), not only prevents the condition but, in certain cases, can be curative.

Pyometra

This literally means "pus in the womb" and is not an uncommon condition in unneutered older bitches. Usually occurring about a couple of months after being in season, early signs often include an increased thirst and urination, with vomiting and a disinclination to eat. Again, urgent veterinary attention is necessary. The condition is usually treated surgically and is obviously prevented if the bitch is neutered.

Having now come to the end of this chapter, you will have some idea of the preventive care requirements, first aid, and common medical problems associated with Jack Russells. Just make sure you enjoy the company of this lively little terrier to the fullest.